Choir of the Wells

Also by Bruce Bond

Choir of the Wells

A Tetralogy

BRUCE BOND

etruscan press

Etruscan Press
Wilkes University
84 West South Street
Wilkes-Barre, PA 18766
(570) 408-4546

WILKES UNIVERSITY

www.etruscanpress.org

Published 2013 by Etruscan Press
Printed in the United States of America
Design by Julianne Popovec
Cover art by Deborah Davidson
The text of this book is set in Crimson.

First Edition

13 14 15 16 17 5 4 3 2 1

Publisher's Cataloging-in-Publication
(Provided by Quality Books, Inc.)

Bond, Bruce, 1954-
    Choir of the wells : a tetralogy / Bruce Bond. -- 1st
ed.
    p. cm.
    Poems.
    ISBN 978-0-9839346-5-3

    I. Title.

PS3552.O5943C46 2013   811'.54
                    QBI13-600015

Please turn to the back of this book for a list of the sustaining funders
of Etruscan Press.

For my friends and teachers, long dead,
with eyes to read what I read in them.

Choir of the Wells

THE BURNING CASKET

I.

II.

III.

WATER SCRIPTURE

I.

II.

III.

EARTH'S APPRENTICE

I.

II.

III.

HOMAGE TO PHOSPHORUS

I.

II.

III.

Acknowledgments

The author would like to thank the following journals in which the poems first appeared:

Alaska Quarterly Review
The Remorse of Narcissus
Zero

Agni
Elegy for the Spanish Republic
Asylum

The Antioch Review
Salt
The Unfinished Slave

The Asheville Poetry Review
Jon Faddis and the High Note

Bellevue Literary Revue
Tinnitus

Beloit Poetry Journal
Audubon

The Boiler Review
Four Preludes for the Choir of the Wells

Borderlands
Energeia

Callaloo
Homage to Lead

Cave Wall
Ground Zero

Colorado Review
Crossfire
Pill

Connecticut Review
Echo

The Cortland Review
Shutter

Crab Orchard Review
The Ghost of Weather
Ice
The Invention of Fire

The Dark Horse
The Listening Chamber

Denver Quarterly
Ode to a Shadow Puppet
Once

Epoch
The Shore

The Fiddlehead
Acolyte
Agoraphobia
Cezanne's Doubt
The Collector
Yedid Nefesh

The Florida Review
Pledge

Gettysburg Review
The News

The Guidebook
Branch
Dirt
Eden

Harvard Review
Robitussin

Hayden's Ferry Review
Homage to Phosphorus

IO: A Journal of New American Poets
Fiat Lux
A Little History of Waves
Saturn

The Journal
Hendrix
Mysterium

Root
Water

Poetry Northeast
One
Wind

Poetry Northwest
Graviton
Survivor

Prairie Schooner
Homage to Sebastian Stenzel
The Lost Year

Quarterly West
Tusk

Raritan
The Blindness of Needles
Ink
The Invisible Hand

Rattle
Boo

River Styx
Garnet
Siren

Salmagundi
The Los Angeles River

Salt Hill
The Fire Eater

Sewanee Review
Limestone
Memento
Pieta

Shenandoah
Seed

Smartish Pace
Marble
Sand

The Southern Review
Convalescence
Cyclops

Southwest Review
Tropical

Stand
Luminescence of the Oceans
Tympanum

Tampa Review
Map

Third Coast
Water Scripture

32 Poems
Carbon
Crown
Winter

Verse
Shine

Volt
Reincarnation

Waccamaw
Nest

Writer's Bloc
Bridal
Camouflage

In addition, the poem "Pill" was featured in *Best American Poetry 2012*; the poem "Benthos" won The New South Poetry Prize; the poem "Horn" was reprinted by *Arcadia;* and "Jon Faddis and the High Note" received a William Matthews Poetry Prize from *The Asheville Poetry Review*. "Audubon" was featured by *Poetry Daily*, and "The Ghost of Weather" was featured by *Verse Daily*. An author's essay and web discussion about the poem "Audubon" can be found at *The Beloit Poetry Journal* website. Also "Water Scripture" and "Echoes of a Lost Tongue" were republished by *The Adroit Journal*. The poem "The Unfinished Slave" is forthcoming in *Best American Poetry 2013*.

Choir of the Wells

THE BURNING CASKET

We all walk on water, now and then,
though it takes the eyes of wells to see it.
When a man's sleep breaks in half, he steps
drunkenly across the blackened surface.
Father, are you there. Can you answer.
Forever a depth that sings beneath our feet.

I.

Luminescence of the Oceans

There is a drowned fire in our leaving.
You see it in the wakes of ships that cut
a passage through the red tide, the sparks

thrown aft as they welter in the current.
Sometimes when I look down at the seeds
of light, I keep returning to the furrow

that made a stranger of my father's body,
the way he slept beneath the surgeon's lance,
the saw, the red hand that reached inside

to turn the organ over. Sleep or no sleep,
a literal heart fumbles with the things
it cannot say and so it says again.

Look at waves. They fold into themselves
the sob of oceans, like a frightened child.
You would think they get tired of it,

how, as they heave exhausted to the bed
of sand, the last remains of day crackle
in the fall. I talk about my father

because, beyond the obvious, I am
afraid the water will swallow him again.
When I look ahead, I see something

futureless there, the jewel of the star
that drizzled into his eye that day.
It seems so still, though I know better.

The machinations of the ocean break
into the million small decisions of the deep.
It lives to move. The star that dissolves

against the foam, it goes somewhere. It must.
Beneath the widow's lace, perhaps, or here
inside the gaze that reads. It spreads its net.

Benthos

The fathoms take what we know of light,
the ache of it that dims as it goes
cold, deeper into the ache of dark.

Down here an eye is its own lantern,
sunk among the cuttlefish and squid,
the angel flesh that swims among the wreckage.

Today I walked into a small museum.
On a wall, a hill of spectacles,
teeth, a memoir bound in human skin.

I have read this book, skin to skin,
and yet I think a part of me reads it
in the dark. If this is the past,

it is far too tiny and too enormous.
What you make out in the many faces
gets lost in the unspeakable focus

of one. And each one difficult to name,
to recognize now, beneath the mask
of no mask. Not enough food to live,

and too much to die. That's what they say.
And it goes on that way for a while,
until the story of the boy who begs

to be shot. The core of us is strange.
Bones of faces float to the surface.
And deeper still, a voice, neither theirs

nor ours. Like a heavy net of cautions
that binds us to a world. Perhaps a prayer,
a memoir's future tense, or the last

breath of a man, here, high above the dark
floor, above the drowned, as we know them,
the gas blue eel, our black and silent stars.

Ink

When, in the dark ages of the east,
the Mongols took the heart of the city
and poured in, room after room, to cut
a path through the bodies in their way,
they loaded up the illuminated books,
the many wildflowers of Islam hand-sewn,
penned, edged in gold, and made of them
a bridge across the Tigris, shaky at best,
to lead men from the spoils of their labor.
This is the story of the House of Wisdom,
how centuries gathered there to pool
the gems of medicine and metaphysics,
until the river took them, leaving us
the ache of knowing just enough to ache.
If history repeats, it does so without us.
It returns the way a criminal returns,
or a tongue to the space that was a tooth.
When the bodies of the philosophers
broke the surface, they floated here and there,
littering the shore, their wounds drained
into the current, to stain the glass
not red exactly, in spite of what you hear,
but rust, a fading scar of dirt and iron.
The greatness of a city is how it kneels
near the water, to beat its laundry there,
or flood the fields in their season, to carry
what: fennel, flax, cinnamon, a scholar.
Beyond the necessary, a river draws
the mourner toward something she cannot find—
it helps her nonetheless—or the believer
toward reconciliation with her god.

If we hear there rumors of water going
on without end, it is none the less loss
that speaks. What book would not be a bridge.
Or the grave of some sad misconception.
Somewhere still there is a volume that says
what the river of the dead cannot,
that once a library fell into the Tigris,
and these waters, that are a widow's friend,
ran black with ink, mile after mile.

A Little History of Waves

I used to think the past was a god
laid to rest in the graves of books
that no one reads, in a paradise
where the quiet is so absolute
no body drums a passage through the page.

All those nights I lost going down
to the shore, when I walked alone
beside the gardens gone sweet with dark,
I left something of a story behind
my words to tell it. Even now I live

where I can never be, though I see
in my many mistakes along the way
the angel of a death that weighs my heart
against the feather of a better life.
Today I learned a friend of mine is dying.

It's something so rare he lived with it
for years, unknowing, so now he has two,
maybe three, to watch his choices narrow
to the repertoire of miracles
that move an arm, an eye, a diaphragm.

Perhaps it is the free movement of things
that first persuades us they are deserving
of a name. Before they can belong
to a world, they belong to themselves,
bound, as we say, to change position

like something that has not happened yet.
I am sending out a prayer, unsure
it goes anywhere at all, let
alone all the way there, beyond the meat
and fear that hold a body to its bones.

Somewhere in my memory I help
the pieces of a man around, thinking
what this place needs is a little light.
So much time to wonder where we are,
or were, or hope we will have been, until

the skies disconnect their constellations
and plunge, released, nameless to the sea.
There is no shepherd of the stars.
Every breath we take they rise
and fall. Less a particle, more a wave.

The Los Angeles River

Hopeful at best this name we give it,
this trickle that is largely a river
of concrete now, a barren culvert

for the flash of floods that shiver
through the city, that come to clean
their gathering here, their never

sublime, never flourishing stream.
Small, yes, but stream enough to slow
down grids of traffic, the limousine

as it rolls its mirror windows,
one side fire, the other ice.
Valley of the winter rose,

of a sage and palm tree paradise
so sun-rich a nation leaned west
to watch, to tap the orange trees

and television glass, the want
that gushed like a would-be starlet.
Valley of the ancient freeways.

And on its banks a palimpsest
of swastikas and bodiless
cocks, the bored, pissed, obsessed

confessions, giant names that last
night trashed beneath another fist
of paint, its flash, its fume, its luster.

Ask the man who sits and finds
comfort here, whose respite is
the rainbow of the river surface.

Sure, a certain shine persists
in the eyes of makeshift families
that comb the night, that climb this fence

because it's there, because the homeless
runoff of a city flows somewhere,
if not to the sea, then to some place

with bridges, echo chambers that water
the sea, that voice whatever talk
of rain. And the rains that answer.

Fiat Lux

In Memory of Joseph Marino

Call it a leak in last night's dream,
where you jump in to save the dog
drowning in a street of water,
only to find yourself pulled under
where the force of sleep opens your eye.
And as you lie awake a moment,
housed in rain, it is a friend
and not a dog you think of, or both,
the way sun is both the gift
of sight and what burns our sight away.
If light is spirit, dark is meat.
Each alone is blindness.
Moreover, the law of measures
tells you, when two occupy one
space, a certain weight of being
divides itself between them.
Such is grief's logic, the geometry
of prayer. Take my friend.
When his body arrived at the altar,
they sprinkled him with faith
in a dead ancestral language.
His father's faith. Not his.
He who gave his flesh to his flesh
and so departed. Some nights still
I am looking for the dog.
Or is it the dog who is looking.
Here boy, I call, which is not his name. Here.

Water

Say you stare into a river
as if this were the way to cure
your madness, your gaze
fixed on some bearing there,
some dead branch where it spears
the glass, so quick to mend,
or the tremor of a first star
the current rocks to sleep.
Say you kneel to admire
the rudderless boats of leaves,
the lightness of the touch
that bears them up, and the faith
they take in the bending
of the water, given over
to the enormous longing below,
its gravity, its give and take,
the sure, swift eddies that spin them
toward some foreign shore.
It's as if the stream came this far
to teach you something,
that there is always more
to strip you, bearing down,
as if the flow could be a sister
stillness, like the stare
beneath the closed eyes
of someone sitting, following
her breath, steadfast there
in letting go. Clouds leave
no ripple in their wake.
And you just might find yourself
where the crackle of water

is a fire you sleep by. It leads you
everywhere and nowhere
like dark traveling into the dark.
And you begin to believe
you were born for this,
to wake, alone, the orphan
of your dreams. You start to see
what's left of night drawn
over the horizon—a tide
that consumes some other east,
some other west, that pulls
the pale blue this way, to float
the burning casket of the sun.

II.

Echoes of a Lost Tongue

1. Oleander

Inside every flower is another,
white mostly, ghost white, blood red, and somewhere
in between, the tiny bead of pollen

a word on its tongue, the kind that means
something near to mind and yet beyond it,
too close in fact, like a blurry object,

the mere scent of meaning calling out
to bees in the language of their instinct.
What lies outside their cipher for the blossom

is the poison there, what feeds the stem,
what nourishes the flower in our gaze.
And so we stop like clocks *to contemplate*,

as we put it, though there is less and less
at the farthest reaches of the poisonous
a bloom cannot articulate more clearly.

Still the blush that rises from the leaves
that kill is somehow wedded to our will
to speak, to hurl a mirror through the world

beyond us, knowing losses ever phantom
these petals, this slowly whitening perfume.
All across the neighborhood, the flowers

ache with a light they cannot capture,
made up of what they forfeit to the day.
Mirror, mirror, if what the skeptics say

is true, that the power of what we see
lies in the beholder, then tell me why
a drop of sap will paralyze the eye.

2. Correspondence

When I was small I believed numbers
had colors that brightened when I closed my eyes,
the hazel of each iris mirrored back

as the shaded fountain of a zero.
And when I opened each O to the world,
I saw a garden, and thought little wonder

people get married in a place like this.
If some poor soul nods off in his tally,
can you blame the force of tedium

that abandons the pale task before him.
What we lack in bewilderment,
we take to a park, to the great weave

of wind and lawn the caretaker tends.
A stone angel kneels over numbers
laid to rest, gone dark green with rain.

Birth minus death, they say, fading.
Numbers are discrete and so shared
the ways colors might be, though no one knows.

They say blood is a different shade
on the inside, though how anyone
discovered this is beyond the reach of light.

When you blush is it a hidden life
that surfaces like autumn in the leaves.
Overhead, you hear the scissors of wings

cut the sky to a million pieces.
One plus one plus one, until, forever,
and the feathers of the song turn blue.

3. Watering the Mirror

It can last for years, the phantom ache
of the hand that is not there, that grips
nothing now and goes on gripping it,

as if in letting go that part of us
would die at last. And then it came, a cure.
With a simple mirror in the place

of the lost hand, you can create another,
a twin, free to move, to slip the image
of its ghost inside the living sleeve.

The eye heals. We know that. Who cares
if what we see are shadows, if deception
turns to faith like an addict in prayer.

Vision travels at the speed of angels,
of all that arrives before doubt can break it.
I have so much to learn, to unlearn again,

as I step from bed into one more day
to shoulder the weight of missing things.
In my garden is a pool that looks

to the sky and what the sky makes out
is the same blue gift the sea and heaven
keep exchanging. No beginning, no end.

When my friend died, he opened up
his arms, like a bird who carried on
for miles without disbelief or movement.

What I see of him I see alive
between an earth and sky that know nothing
of each other and, as mirrors, nothing but.

One

Today the heavy snow makes difficult
the roads, and I touch the glass to test
the cold, to teach myself how to face it.

You loved that, how clarity relieves
the burden of the clear. One day you woke
to the thought your life was not your life

alone. But whose. The tap of the distant
faucet was never more insistent, the way
it gave a name to the quiet around it.

When they found your body, it sizzled with flies.
Dead letters in your mailbox, the body's
little debts whose total was enormous.

When I pass the dumpsters on Frye Street,
I smell the last good cigarette snuffed
in wine. Not you. But a sacrament of you,

a shadow lost to a confluence of shadows.
Language has no body, and so you loved
to liken it to one. As if talk were enough

and bodies born of it. That's one way
to mend the rift between us and a world
that was fine before we came, and so continues.

It lightens things, true, the thought we lose
our singularity just looking around,
every window a page the snow revises.

You said to me, you know a language is
dead when it will not tolerate mistakes.
White travels into white. The mail arrives.

I type some letters in the field without
knowing, step by step, and when I turn back,
I vanish, buried in the snow's reply.

Zero

The shape of nothing is unruly
for a child, its curve closed,
complete, though open as an eye.

It is, as such, of two worlds,
the way an eclipse is both
the sun and the cold shadow

that fits perfectly inside it.
So snug, this darkness, this face
laid over the faces we meet.

To return the circle's stare
is to vanish through, to fledge
the watchful target with an arrow.

But the zero keeps the distance
of things so close we cannot see.
Picture a clock. No hands. No ratchet.

No numbers even. How odd
it does not think of itself
as an hour among the hours.

Once I felt a woman's mouth
open against mine, in each
a zero echoed by the other.

I wanted hers the way light
wants a window, a window light,
a voice the space of the unspoken.

Later I woke to the distant
breathing of the waves. Zero
minus zero minus zero.

Without a halo here and there,
how would I number the light
years between here and hereafter.

Some stars went out long ago,
of course, and yet they slip through
the ring of the human gaze.

When my mother died, her jaw
gaped with a dark song like one
of the choir. None knows the meaning

of our word for what she is.
When I close my eyes I see
it still, her face in the lamplight,

just before I enter sleep.
One, I say, over and over,
as if one plus one were still one.

The Shore

for Clive Wearing

If memory has a center, let it be here.
Unless, that is, a fever takes it, the brain

a hole the size of who we were, or worse,
who we would be, who we are now, or now.

Ask the man inside his small bay window.
Not that his wife is a stranger. Far from it.

If ever she leaves his room a moment,
she returns to him as the long lost face

to a happiness he forgot he had.
And so the art of moving forward, loss

over loss in waves against the shore.
Just listen to his music, the unlikely

way it shivers through him, his language
worn to something crystal in the current.

See his eyes close as his hands begin,
a face afloat the black of his piano.

The deeper he goes, the darker the gloss,
the more sand he lets fall through the hour.

Whatever binds one measure to another,
it binds the damage the way air binds objects

in a room, until one day his wife stops,
transfixed above a sink of dishes, to say,

how strange, I was just about to do that.
A glass chimes in her hand. Then she rinses,

mindful, places it on its mouth to dry.
Each one listening for the next to speak.

Phantom Joy

After the phantom pain fades out
into the common grave of air,
you still may feel a certain presence,

a chill, a curse, and after that
the slow crush of deep exhaustion.
Or entangled in the chronicle

of nerves, you might discover
something older, some ghost core
you call your need to continue,

love you suffered through and for,
the shattered part a monument
razed to open up the view.

Inside the flesh, bone; inside
the bone, the idea of bone,
the will to fashion one, to bind

the urge of the first rogue cell
that hardened into white, pressed
by dread and blind exuberance.

We rise, we walk, in time we run.
Was it to or from some danger
or both at once. What sparked you

on this journey, the heart's bullet
shot out of that particular dark,
though something of the child

you were skeletons your dreams,
or pulls your breath farther inward,
quickened by some sharp pleasure

or scare, some surprise that releases
what's left of you to morning, a stranger
to your nature, to hear there a girl

on a swing, the way she screams
to the chirping of the chains, alive
and falling, merciless and undiscouraged.

The Invisible Hand

Our life has no end the way our visual field has no limits.
— LUDWIG WITTGENSTEIN

Light, we know, is an invisible thing.
The beam that falls through the theaters
of a childhood—we trust it's there

thanks only to the dust that floats inside it,
and the screen, of course, the stuff that takes
the dark of light and makes of it a story.

In this way light provides a language
for the dawn of things, ourselves, for instance,
how we travel through the first two years

into the luminous amnesia of who
we are, blind to the gods of days that made us.
A body might be replaced twelve,

thirteen times over, every cell hung
on the architecture of what goes missing,
the way the widow hangs on her son's arm,

on the strength inside his long black sleeve.
Today I listened to Ravel's *Concerto*
for the Left Hand, to its vague beginnings

in the bass violins, the rocking cradle
of the bow as if it were tuning up
for what's to come, for the slow emergence

of a subject, the polish of the brass,
the great wave that peaks and washes ashore
the hand, the A, the lowest of the keys.

It's the announcement of our soloist
whose body lies buried in the ghost
of sound. Do you think of him as well,

Paul Wittgenstein, the man who lost his arm
to a Russian bullet, how he woke
in a prison hospital to find it gone.

He could not see this yet as the birth
of all the left-hand scores he would commission,
Ravel's, for one. In truth, music's origins

are the casualties of every age.
Given time, days wept a pool of light
over charcoal keys he sketched on a crate.

And as he taught his hand to play the parts
that were not there, the reach of it grew
desperate, quick, as if it were two hands,

worlds apart, one dead, another living,
each one abandoned by the other,
bound by that to the talk between them.

What is more intangible than the past
to come. Remember, him on stage, the tuck
of the sleeve that fluttered in its pins.

I have seen his performance in a movie,
his hand leaping like a bird on fire,
as if all he lost brought on an excess

of life. The madness and the suicides
of a tragic family—they can break you
down or open, or a little of both.

You can almost hear him as he turns
to his brother to say, is it true,
what we cannot speak about we must

pass over in silence. But what if
silence too begins to speak, or sing,
to be the hand that is no longer there.

What if death is dark as any beam
that illuminates a score of music.
Birth too. Or the want to give birth

and so be born. There is no idea
as powerful as the will to have one.
And as the orchestra gathers up

its strength beneath the hand, everything
falls the way a building falls through
blooms of dust. I live for times like that,

for beginnings, ends, the great dark hall
alive and listening, the light we only
know as light the moment that it's broken.

III.

In Memory of Scott Simpkins

Pill

Say you are high all the time save those moments
you take a sobriety tablet and so descend
the nerves of the heart, thinking straight,

they call it, as if the mind were an arrow
shot from the eye into the eyes of others,
the ones you wronged, the ones you never knew

you love or do not love, the black fathoms
of their pupils deepening as your eyes close.
And sure it hurts, how something dead walks out

your sleep, how it goes from blue to red
like blood. And yet the stuff keeps calling you
in a father's voice. You loved your father,

so it's more than bitter seeds you swallow.
It's quiet pleasure within the limitations
of one life, until the great space of a day

gets wider, brighter, as if you were slipping
into summer with its giant measures
of desire, the way just sitting makes it rise.

And yes, with each dose comes the gravity
and boredom, the slow crush of August heat,
though you are learning to live here, in a town

with one good street to speak of, one flock of trees
to storm the night. In time you are addicted.
And it takes more of the drug to get you back

to the world, where morning swallows flit
in last night's rain. In time you tell yourself
you are the age you are: the little pains

inside your arms, your legs, they are just that:
the pinch that says you are not asleep,
that the compulsion you feel is the pull

of the planet you walk, alone. And the dawn,
however deep you breathe, is everyone's now,
everyone's breath in the sky above you,

everyone's sun aching into layers
of mist, spitting fire in the eye,
its one black star dissolving, like a pill.

The Smokers

It goes against our deepest instincts,
the Buddha who, eyes closed, breathes the tar
of another's suffering, then releases

the body's reservoir of light, taking
on a pain that is, by nature, a thing
we cannot take, we cannot take away.

So why bother after all. Why drink
imaginary poison, as if the motions
of life would dust the jewel in our chest.

Perhaps we, who know so little sleep,
glide into a harbor made of fog
and lower anchor there. Take my friend

who grew so weary of the obvious,
who lit one Camel with the last, and yes,
he quit, as if it mattered, as if the final

ditch could save him. His wife quit as well,
late, then took it up again in mourning.
It kept her company, like the scent

that hung among the shirts in her closet.
With every match she cradled, she passed
a torch from one craving to another,

as she did when they first talked, alone,
high on the steps of a small museum.
Just the specks of them and the night sky,

how it glimmered as their embers breathed,
each a momentary pulse, responding,
an ache to feed the sweetness of the smoke.

The Fire Eater

You see it in the eye of all
who stare, the tiny fire eater
and his still more tiny flame,

a star, out there, in the way
gods are, or the child's face
in the well, the mirrored mirror.

Last night I dreamt of a friend
I saw drown himself, drink
by drink, and I asked him how

it was without the sting of it,
the disingenuous laugh that said
nothing, and went on saying it.

The swallower's art is simple.
Heat rises. The rest is pain.
And lies about it. No cold flame.

No tongue anesthetized in ice.
The man with a bottle looks up
into the night to throw it down.

To think we were born of such,
in the combustibles of angels.
Soon enough exhaustion leads us

through a theater of want
we almost take for understanding.
There is no dream for the dreamer.

Only you and the world, feasting
on each other. Then you wake, dry.
We all sleep deepest with our mouths

open. Who on earth are we calling.
And where does it lead, this long
dark throat, this trail of tiny blisters.

Saturn

When you vanish, you are everywhere,
telling me how there is no way back
once you see it, the house of sticks we call
a self, the way it staggers into questions
of power, open spaces, fists of dust.

What is an addict but a constructivist,
permissive as any prostitute or child,
any face blurred at the bottom of a glass.
As you brace against the bar door, do you
step into its shadow, you the offspring

of your great amnesia, those years lost
to what, you cannot tell, though you see it
as a god, a father, a freak of nature.
Perhaps it is the nightmare Goya painted
on a wall of the Villa of the Deaf,

the appetite that ate its son. Why is it
the eyes of the patriarch open widest
when they are most blind, most voracious.
Is the heart disfigured with shame a house
of sticks, the black context of the near

there to crumple up the body to a roar.
Pity, as you know, does not make a monster
any less. There are bottles of blood
and worry I long to drain. That said,
it's the kind of painting you would love.

Inside the hole that bears the memory
of the head, there is a boy who sees
nothing, as if that too were a hole, a mouth,
as if the gods and fathers that consume us
are the ones we will not, cannot, know.

Mysterium

What name do you give the cat
who strangely no friend knew by name,
who paced your small house gone
dark for days until they found you.

It must be out there somewhere,
the name that is a piece of you
and yet not you, the way a thought
is never the mind that thinks it.

And so I hunt among the dead
philosophers, my thick hardbacks,
and find a flaw, a set of black
jackets with a gap in the middle.

That too is thick, the missing book
I loaned you, and as your cat
looks up, bewildered, nameless still,
I see in him the absent pages.

A book about the art of healing,
how those who would be whole tear
through some necessary wound,
cut from the mess, and so related.

Sam, I thought. I will name him
after the author of *Kubla Kahn*,
with its pleasure dome, sad lute,
eyes blurred with opium and pollen.

It is a place you understood,
too well, I fear, the cold fountain
where it sizzled in its spoon.
Truth is, I hate the pretense of pets

with literary credentials, and yet
what is better than the story
of this poem, the knock on the door
that broke the writer's delirium,

that cut his vision short, to say,
there is a world here, remember,
a dawn that is the tomb of sleep.
Not long ago you and I met

over coffee, our morning meal,
unaware we were leveling
the ground between us for a name
to lie over the one we'd lose.

Sam noses under the book
I am reading and so lay down.
We are many people, you said,
therefore, I imagine, many graves.

My Death Space Dot Com

Now that obituaries come online
with coroner reports and full disclosure,
imagine the ways to betray a man
come out of hiding to die. Ask the bloggers
who weigh in on my friend's bad habit,
who make of it their own drug strung out
across a mirror, so when they pay tribute
to their power, how they had their doubts
about his talent, his flu, I think how lucky
I was to receive the kindness of the weak.
My death space, as they call it, as if it's me
who died. A life, we know, is complex.
But death is simple. A place to talk shit,
to license grief, or barring that, to kill it.

Robitussin

The boy who stood, patient, alone,
outside my night class in the cold,
who waited out the hangers-on
who held me with their final questions,
or shyly handed me their drafts,
the waver of their long hand.
The boy who watched the others
step against their cigarettes and break
their conversations, him there
half-hidden by the trees, hands
in pockets as if to clutch a coin in each.
The boy who followed me stair
by stair to the dim confessional
that was my office, walled in the faces
of friends and teachers, long dead,
with eyes to read what I read in them.
We were just a bunch of lonely boys,
he said. And then the furtive
details, the four bottles a night,
the syrup in his bones, how the high
was a bit like codeine at first,
then turned visionary, dire. Weird,
he said, and then again, having arrived
at that place where words sink
back into the throat that made them.
And I saw him on some gated dock
in Houston, gazing through the empty
bottle at the light of a ship
in the distance. He had that pallor
that was half-alive, half-angelic,
and that glass heart of the addict,

the sense he saw something in that ship
neither approaching nor drifting off,
just a bobbing in the malaise that was
the waters of the bay. Lonely boys,
he called them, the dispossessed
who slipped their vial of shame
and excitement from a bag,
their pupils wide with the night's
great and empty spaces. What
do you say to a boy whose head
bows at land's end, that it's true,
that suffering teaches nothing,
not mere suffering, suffering alone,
however far it hopes to take you
past the sour dumpsters
through the shooting galleries
of harbor towns moaning like ships.
Not the gulf refineries that puzzle
the sky, the way the floodlight
on their bones guides a vandal
through the fences, through eyes
that only a child can thread.
Some boys are boys forever
staring out at the black tanker
carving forward, sluggish and deep,
the rainbow of the engine's
water streaming out for miles.
Not suffering alone, but the long
negotiation of days to follow.
Which is why he was there
after all, the boy in my office.

Surely there is virtue in the invitation,
in the word that hallucinates
the child who fell asleep
with a ruby of poison by his heart.
Imagine the flash of the prow
that cuts the mind like bread,
that says, this is my body. Come.
Eat. Eat and be whole again.
Drink until your feet dangle off
the edge of the landing and walk.
A ship named *Lost* chafes
at its anchor. A searchlight dims.
Gods lean down in their bodies
made of emptiness and fire:
tomorrow, tomorrow. Tonight
I am grateful to the language
that elevates a boy stair by stair,
to the inexpressible that begins
the journey. I am grateful
to the flesh that dissolves
into words, which in turn longs
for the flesh once more, the stranger
a child curls inward to comfort,
to survive, to carry home, to be there
in the end, no child at last,
no harbor friend beside him as he wakes.

Echo

When I speak, I am spoken, each word
a mouth of words that stretch into the distance.
I am not alone. I had a friend once
with whom, mornings over coffee, I grew
so comfortable, we slipped in and out
of books and the voices that would read them.
It always felt different in the air,
each solitude an understanding and thus
not absolute. So in the end, when his voice
abandoned his body for good, I heard it break
into a flock of voices. All night they beat
the wings of the near at hand: the clock,
the pen, the iPhone with his name inside.
Some seemed to flutter out of the earth,
to storm the mantle from below, or thump
the great door of my bed, until, facedown,
at last, I opened. And the silence answered.

WATER SCRIPTURE

Not that he expected a reply, not yet.
But something in the spirit of the question
as it dug its oracle, its grave, its worldly
passage, saw the art of it, not in the hole,
but in the earth that flew upon the surface.

I.

Water Scripture

It takes two brains to dream about a brain,
to fathom the confusion inside a man
I know, how he looks at words and sees

not words exactly but little pictures,
snips of thread. And yes, he sees them
clear enough; he writes them even,

though only when he closes his eyes,
his hand given over to what he cannot
read, clarified by darkness like a star.

Perhaps it is not so useless, the myth
of the eye that casts the movie of the world
on the back of the brain, though who,

I wonder, would be there in the theater
to watch. Is his eye too a projector,
his skull a screen, and on it goes, down

to the eye of the nucleus inside him,
to the last small witness, the tiny god
of seeing, what sees itself being seen.

There are those who believe that god
created us so she might know her nature,
that she inks her pen in us, we who write

inside the blackout of our theater,
alone, not quite ourselves, and yet refreshed,
our eyes the spectacles of other eyes.

So many quiet deaths along the way,
it's hard to fathom what we offer heaven
in the end, if there's a waiting room

for all our castaways: the severed leg,
the strength we lost, the broken molecules
of thought, before we lost our train of thought.

If the head is a garden, who walks
the path, who lifts the tiny latch, making
music across the little gaps of mind.

Nerves flash and we see red, or dream it,
though who fires the nerve, let alone
takes note, what homunculus stares

into the blaze. The gates click open and sing.
Years from now, when our words break
down across the coals, do we hurry

to finish passages we cannot read.
When I think of my friend's brain, the movie
of the visible lodged in its projector,

how the tumor eats into the middle
of the story, I keep seeing the white
eye, the screen behind the universe,

revealed, not as what he interprets,
but more as a release, a gift, a morning
sun the watchman drives through into sleep.

A body understands. It moves about
as freely as a body will allow.
And as its choices dwindle, the darkening

context brings it closer to the movie.
To be taken out, and yet remain,
to be the tooth aching in its socket,

once, it seemed, I wanted nothing more.
In the garden of the black umbrellas,
I stared into a hole filled with rain,

whispered to the makeshift oracle,
inarticulate with prayer, and I forgot
myself a moment, my place inside

the soundtrack, its arc, its end, its mission.
One cruel awakening deserves another,
said the sky. The mind creates mind,

said the earth. And both seemed equally
true, in spite of death's slow appetite
for who we are, we were, what we fathom.

The man inside the man inside, and so on,
who's to say it does not go on this way,
while we're alive at least, we who watch

the fire of the human heart sizzle
in the well. Ever to write the passages
we cannot read, not knowing what a brain

knows. Not to mention the hand, the one
that misses us, cut off, it seems, abandoned
to the blindness of our study. I hear it

as it scribbles in grief back to the body.
From the world I came and so return, it writes,
in its own dark way embedded, free.

Yedid Nefesh

As a child I thought sleeping on my left
spilled the skyward contents of my brain
in a trickle of blood and intuition,
a rain so tentative it made no sound.
It gave sleep weight, depth, engendering
the indiscernible seeds of life that pools
engender, until my head slowly evolved
into a planet, a child's, granted, but sure
to lose the swimmer to the shore, the lamb
to the lion, the sparrow to the open sky.

And so in time one half of me returned
to the other something of the wine
that pours out the bottle of the heart
into one of those late night confessions
among friends, however estranged by loss
and betrayal, however laid bare
to partial misconceptions that cut deep
into the black origins of morning.
A record needle lifts as the two part,
taking something of the music with them.

Tonight my wife sings a Hebrew prayer,
our dog, as he howls, blind with something:
some wound of pleasure, or want, or both at a once.
Just who he calls to is anyone's guess.
And in that moment as I lift my head
from an open book, I sense the smallest
laughter in her note, not music merely,
but a ripple in the surface where the cry
goes under, a shimmer I close my eyes to hear
clear from the darkest corner of our house.

Crush

In this dream he is the deep-sea diver
going down with his hypnotist, the ocean
body blue with cold, with a shiver
of flashlight pale and fading, digging in.

Three thousand feet. And still I keep seeing
them as astronauts of the underworld,
grown shadowless, bodiless, it seems,
and yet, what could be more fiercely willed

than breathing, more guarded than the angel
of our lungs. More near. The farther from home
the closer the chest; the tighter the skull,
the mask, the mortal circle. Look at him:

the way he hesitates, interring fathom
after fathom. Three thousand pounds above
both him and the one who counsels him,
or so he believes, being neither brave

nor sure of the deepest cliffs, the drone
beneath his small uneasy life. No sand
to breach, to shape, to lay his head on. *Go on,*
says the hypnotist, eager to proceed,

swollen with the progress they have made.
Such revelations like coins inside the water
of the hour, the exotica of the mind's mind,
defenseless, manic, burning with dark matter.

And in days that follow, the patient shuns
all glances but his own, dips in the black
target of his gaze, blind with visions,
swallowed in the spell that will not break.

Three thousand feet. Ask any diver in the flesh.
The dream knows, being water. Close, closer.
Look at his hands. The more they take the less
they hold. They too begin to talk, to quiver.

What do I say to them, once the blood rushes
to the center. Who will look after this cloud
when it fractures, when the tanks are crushed;
what darkened eye not knowing if it's closed.

The Island

Once it was a buried mountain,
a red gash in the ocean floor,
the pressure of the liquid stone
surging upward as it flared

the way anger flares, amorphous
first, then cold, black, in time hard,
deep beneath the steaming surface.
For all we know, it went unheard

by boats that hurled their harpoons
in peace, apprenticed to their needs,
as slowly fire parted the wound
where it was oldest, where it bled

into the landscape of the waves.
That too was made of molten glass,
brightened by a sun that wove
a chain of light across the place.

All night the rock boiled its soot
with all the urgency and risk
of lives that crawl from the planet,
that would fix their grip on this

world, as if there were no other.
And as the conflagration freed
a cloud of sulfur into the air,
it likewise spilled a mercury

of blessings over fertile ground,
the aphid, the cricket, the green flame
of grass, the harvest of the gods.
Although the island took its name

from us, we felt a certain lack
of entitlement. What luck,
to live in the wind that clacks
these sails into a gentle panic.

To the corpses washed ashore,
tell them this, that their past
has carved our hearts into a harbor.
Or to the stranger if she asks,

say that once an island cast
its net into the sea's cauldron,
a writhing in the tide, the ash
of thousands in the seeds of rain.

Awakenings

1. Seed

The seedling as it shatters into life
casts a tangled shadow. Root by root
it digs and in its digging lifts its knife
into the air, blind, wary, drowned in light.

Even the dead inside the soil grip
the earth the way a mother grips an arm,
a chair, a trusted thing to help her up.
Take these flocks of corn kept from harm

by tall trees that flutter as they bend.
A shiver runs from earth to sky, sky to earth,
the planet's nerves flashing in the wind.
Once I dreamt in the color of my breath

a host of branches sprouted from my lips.
When I woke, their blush had come and flown.
There're words for this, beyond my fingertips.
I've known bare limbs in the lake below,

wreathed in algae, buried in their own sky.
They vein the gaze of the grieving widow,
an open grave in the lake of her eye,
black and shining, bristling with the lost world.

2. The Listening Chamber

Say you discover you have rented a room
to a woman you never see but know
by voice, the kettle's cry, a hurried broom,
the stench of something burning on the stove.

And as your heart beats, so too the wall
that carries the bass of an angry music.
And it goes on this way, the rise and fall
of each curse half-unspoken, the click

of stilettos, the pecking of a key,
until the near stranger becomes more strange
for being near, more buried in the history
that is yours now, or so you imagine.

Each night is more disturbing than the last.
Still you teach your mind to slow, to listen,
to be the surgeon's hand that makes its cut
toward some suffering it cannot dwell on.

Which is when it comes, the shriek, the flare,
sounds of teeth eating through the furniture,
the rented room in flames you break through
to save her, as she, on fire, breaks into you.

3. Heat

We called it the other winter, the wave
that rolled over our lives, withering our lawn,
our sleep, our appetite, the clay foundation
of our home. We called it all that weighed

on us, those days a heavy sickness swept
my wife's womb and took us down a street
that had no shade, save inside our moments
of small jokes, songs, whatever we'd invent

to keep the light from blackening our meals.
Those were the widest days of the year,
the full blow of sunshine most everywhere
we wandered. Parked cars cracked beneath their shields.

And though the long awaited news saved
her, saved us, something stayed behind,
something even in the storm, the cloud
that breezed at last through the open sleeve.

Some thunder broke the circle of the eye,
our refuge darkly fragile with the grief
of the womb, lost now, beneath the roof
that sizzled as we woke, burning and alive.

4. Agoraphobia

Early, as the world returns, I listen
to the tumbling machinery of stars,
a horn, a cat, the clash of a dumpster,
a crackle of hammers on the pale horizon.

Now and then a siren cuts our street
along the sternum, down lanes of strangers
beneath the mask of the morning paper,
above the grate that shudders at their feet.

A city has its reasons to be cautious,
to greet each visitor through the hole
in its door, to latch and bolt the child
that is a body, and more so as it ages.

Not to blame the malice and ache of space,
but more this desire to be there,
to look down from the glass elevator
and see myself in the growing distance.

So if I hold my arms in my arms,
do not say I hate the world. Alone,
hell, it's all I think of, what I smother
in bed. And as I fall, a window opens.

Masters of the Plein Air

Go ask the sun on each horizon.
The child counts her age in days,
months. The older man shortens
up his steps, leaning forward,
blown backward by the light ahead.
I have seen him in his barn
gather up a small bouquet
of brushes drying in a jar,
then make it out into the meadow
when daybreak swells like a coal
beneath the breathing of the wind.
Already the leaves of the parched
elms cast their small flotilla
of blues and grays, where he plants
his easel in a wave of grass,
his art the single island there,
the one still thing in a sea of things.
From the steeple down the valley,
a distant bell marks the hour
the way a buoy marks the buried
hazards of the reef below.
What, he thinks, did he expect,
that clocks would look to him all day.
He works against time, against
the sun even, and yet indebted
to both, to the very swift
that rakes these shadows down
the open country to the west.
His eyes are nothing alone, not
without the thick spectacles
that make them large, though partly

cloudy as the morning is.
Still he sees what remains
of sunlight and the year to come
as an homage to the many
speeds of radiance. Thank
the masters of the *plein air*,
he thinks. What better than to paint
ten unfinished canvases
a day until each at its hour
comes into focus. Even now
the color of midnight blends
into the foliage of his palette
the way a mourner's veil blends
into the dawn of what she sees.
The day ahead grows long, longer.
A breakfast bell rings for him.
Where better to wait than here,
in the stream of shadows across
his shoes. Every light a twilight.

II.

Asylum

After Lyonel Feininger

Picture a dark fugue of interiors,
and there in each the long slits of windows
as imagined from the outside—an alley,

or the many versions of an alley,
as if the city fell from a great height
and shattered strangely, neatly into shards,

so what you get is a universe,
ordered, yes, but whose violence
of accident yields a certain hope,

a play, where tiny brushstrokes of no
one shade tell us there is freedom here.
And at the corner of our sanctuary

looking in, a man, the only stain
of red, poised to enter the solitary
gate, to dwindle like a prayer, a flame.

It is 1914. The alley narrows.
The prow of it cuts a sea of clouds.
And if you look hard, the night suggests

some rough shape at the vanishing:
a second man perhaps, his back to us,
a soldier, a thief, or just a superstition,

a hole at the tapering end of things.
Perhaps the shadow of our protagonist,
a charred fragment, having wandered off

into the distance, swallowed by the maze.
Picture happiness here, the painter said,
I do, though who among us wouldn't pour

through all these unlit windows, these cracks
in joy, careful to keep our voices low
as if history were out there, lightly sleeping.

Take me with you, says the red to the black.
Somewhere the distant cannons of the storm.
Take me, says the fire to the smoke,

the man to the shadow, the one who sees us,
flees us, leads us on, the one whose face
keeps disappearing the moment that he turns.

The Blindness of Needles

After Goya

When a maker of images goes deaf,
he sees a world clarified by silence,
a lens wept over the things unspoken.
Doubtless this is why we find the man
facedown on a drawing table, hands
on his head to shelter him from flocks
that feast on sleep. The blood in his hair,
the lynx, the bats, more than beast, less
than human, all dark fuel for the lantern.
The etcher's needle shines as it cuts.
It takes enormous care, to draw the curve
of a manacle, to rust it shut,
not with neglect, but with the precision
of a scar. Night sweeps the avenues
into brothels, asylums. These sure proportions,
they give to nightmare a logic, an edge
to deepen the line where the acid pours.
Across the cobblestones of Madrid,
lamps beat the laundry of their shadows.
The hearts of the city loosen their fists.
If reason sleeps, as the etching says,
it dreams. Like any theater, the blacker
the wings, the more fiercely we believe.

John Cole and the Waterfall

So when he paddled to the waterfall
in his small boat, he set up his easel
in the bow, the oars at either side
the wings of a gull at rest in flight,
and he began to look, for hours he looked,

at the fine print of the open book
of leaves, their broken binding, the page
of color beneath the page, beneath the plunge
that seeks the low with a kind of longing
insurgency, as if to look this long,

this hard, was to peel away the skin
of light, to reveal the blackening
tension and straight white lines, the will
to resist, to live, here, where all things fall
through nature's hourglass. A painter paints

a floating path against the elements,
against the welter of the thunderhead
and impetuous surge, what led
his boat downstream, in its hull a mirror
of rain, a palette that the clouds smeared

as it shattered through. And he thought less
of his own fate than that of the canvas
laid beneath his jacket, the child he fathered
on its way out of the swollen river,
out of the challenge of water against rock.

The sticks of oars shuddered in their locks.
And though the sky hung low and opened,
the labor of the hours remained, pinned
alive beneath the torrent, above the splash,
though to his mind never finished, a patch

of canvas untouched where the river fell.
Which is how he liked it, the invisible
now a point of entry, a swift to pull
the eye and all that was in it, to hurl
the sky's increasing window to the world.

Shutter

There's a quality of legend about freaks.
Like a person in a fairy tale who stops you
and demands that you answer a riddle.
                              —Diane Arbus

When the flash goes off we go blind,
given over to a place made possible
by blindness. Light overflows the eye

as if to clarify the dark we see with.
It's all a lie of course. We know that.
We flinch at the sting of the shutter,

snap our lid the instant of the shot.
With all the rude wonder of the literal
heart, they come to greet us: the abject posture

of the giant, the child with a toy
grenade, his face in a seizure of play,
each horror pulled away as it draws

a little closer, into the dead still
solitude of a moment in the past.
What is a photograph if not a window

over a broken clock. All is glass.
Shame and awe. That is what the artist
confesses, bound by this to the mother

of the nine foot man, her face too small
for the eyes inside it, fixed on the freak
that passed through her body to the world.

If this is horror, it is not enough
the echo of our heartbreak makes it so.
Nor can we all be monsters and remain

monstrous. What do we really know.
Once a girl—an orphan of the fur trade,
a father's absence, a mother's nervous break—

grew up to coax the body's camera open
like a stage. The giant in the legend,
if he seems disfigured, perhaps it's nothing

more than the room around him, the mean
confines of the conversation he is in.
Is he not made of distance, of talk

that fades into an effigy of seeing.
Who are we to imagine less, to close
the fist of the iris. Light is gigantic.

To look or not look, choose your self-reproach.
Which says, it was never the act of looking
that mattered. Only the power that bears our shame.

Pieta

Not him, that broken idol of a man,
cradled, mute, serene, a child again,
small inside the deluge of her gown.
Not the ripple of his emergent bones,
the milk of his body poured over hers.
No. It was the figure of the mother
that suffered most, when a geologist
took a hammer to her maiden face
and tore away a nose, a cheek, an arm
no less, before the church guards pulled him
down. *I am Christ Jesus,* he cried,
risen from the dead. And who could deny
the faith it took, the insurgent spirit,
the cold place he shattered to release it.
Christ come to part the feminine
tide that washes over everything,
the anima mundi, the virgin and her one
disciple chiseled of the same stone.
It's what binds those who pause, look,
whisper a little, lost inside the rock
made heavy with her garment, its burial
of grief that animates the beautiful.
Hell is other people, say the only
children of the Lord. And it's lonely,
the hell it takes to strip away the skin
on its throne, and make it rough again.
A kind of restoration of the blind,
to hammer in rage, desperate to find
that nail, wherever it is, to strike the shadow
from a woman's body, blow by blow.

Cézanne's Doubt

Just days before his last day, he worked
the rough patch around his gardener's head,
the nimbus a thing of gravity, of slate,

bold, yes, and yet the residue of question
after question laid across the wall,
contusion-blue, as the man who posed

with the patience of a rock, a Sainte
Victoire, held something back, as rocks will,
or all such forces of the garden. Elsewhere.

That's how the painter liked it, how he lived
on some far margin of his gift estate.
Which is why it took the hired help

to find him when, too weak to negotiate
the mud and flowers, he fainted in the rain.
Letters from the world, that's what he wanted.

Words out of focus, too near, too far,
or both at once, like an angel of death
watching over flocks of willows at night.

It was his life to keep an eye on things,
drawn to the lamp inside the visible,
inside the mountain face, the one he scaled

down, sixty times and never the same,
the linen of its valleys, its bruises, its lakes,
draped, it seemed, over the head of someone

staring into space. What is obsession
if not the ghost of a childhood fear
that travels all its days, exhausted, to lie

down with lions, to find its flesh at last.
I want give the dread of unlit spaces
this: a window, a moon, an apple to polish

the light that breaks there. Can you blame the man
if he longed to be seen and yet
invisible, a father's shadow falling

through him. Any wonder he would paint
the seed without opening the apple.
All the work he slashed or left undone,

it was the meat he sacrificed to gods
that hungered, alone, the way believers do.
Look, he told himself. Look again.

The eyes of doors close so ours might open.
A half-truth at best. And he knew it.
Look at the gardener there, the self-

sure angle of the soiled coat that tells us
there is an earth behind the face he wears.
But where there is earth, there is weather.

Those hours in bed listening to the trees
of lungs, the wind's final inquisition.
Audacity and doubt, they are one man's

hands that find each other in the dark,
that find himself, not as he was, but as
he must be, like all new things lost a little,

called to the weeds and reaches of a place
that draws him, shivering, step by step,
to part the shattered mirror of the leaves.

The Unfinished Slave

The man we see writhing in the marble,
what is he without the strength of all
we do not see. A slave, we are told,
though to what: the rock, the king, the world
that, cut or uncut, we can't remember.
To be distinct, chiseled as a number
across a grave, that was his dream once.
If only he could shake the rough stone
from his back, instead of being one.
Or if he stood naked before the tomb
he was meant to guard, perhaps then
he would wear a god's glass complexion.
As is, he is abstract, and so closer
to us, to the life that makes a future
the anticipated past, our heads half
buried, blind, disfigured by the stuff
to which we owe our restlessness, our art.
The hand that carves its figure in the slate
abandons it, thinking hands will lie
beneath their work some day, beneath a sky
that refuses to commit, to lift.
It's in there somewhere, whatever's left
of those who drive a hammer into us.
With every blow, a little bloom of dust
flies. Time keeps its promise to itself.

Elegy for the Spanish Republic

No rendering of the appearance of reality can move us
like a revelation of its structure.

         —ROBERT MOTHERWELL

On the other hand there is the body
whose skin draws so tight about the bones
it makes plain the shield across the heart,
which is to say, the decay of anyone,
of nations no less, coaxes to the surface
something bold, impoverished, the infrastructure
that wears our nervous system like a coat.

In a photo made abstract by time,
a soldier props his rifle on the great swell
of a dead horse, finding protection there,
where all flesh is grey, the black salt
of the emulsion eroded by the light.
Death simplifies. Resolves. It pins
one fear to the other in its crosshairs.

Despotic, you could say, though it opens
up a man's gaze, as if in looking hard,
here behind the guardian smoke of homes
on fire, he saw his own cry approaching.
Every soldier is a metaphysician
who sends a bullet through the skin to see
there the deeper workings of a regime.

It takes a workman's brush in the fist
to paint the great bars of a testament
to silence, to the sheer scale of it drawn
over the mouths of those who weigh down
the wagons in the street. Are they jailed there,
these open sores on the canvas, these eyes,
or do they wet the stiffening insistence

of the lines, the arced exclamations,
writ large, bent against the quiet tide.
White, from lead mostly, highly toxic.
Black, from charred bones, horns, even gas.
Together they make a language indelible,
scarred, and yet, it is the gesture we see,
the assertion of a widow's love hurled

at the speed of rage. We do not look
the way we feel, at once enormous and small,
as if we were both the iconography
and its citizen, its eye. A thing, perhaps,
but so too the flash that is the x-ray
of our grief, that strikes a blow in stillness
where the plow of the sternum begins to rise.

III.

Ode to a Shadow Puppet

My hands are not the bird.
What flies flies in light
of what the bird is not.

I move, it moves, and so
in turn we enter the eye's
bottomless well of ink.

At times my fingers work
so long, so hard, they lose
their place in the story.

The pen and the page
beg the question: what
binds them in their progress

if not a thread of shade.
All the little puppets
of puppets know the strange

and necessary freedom
it takes, the original
response. Go on and ask.

As if the hand that plows
the snow of the unwritten
leaves behind a language

to plow the field again.
A word is not a word
therefore, if not borrowed,

worn, abused, beaten
as it beats its wings
into the open. Today

I heard a sparrow speak.
Neither truths nor lies
but nameless. One life, it said,

a call to things not yet
conceived, not yet, like all
dark origins of song.

Survivor

The woman at the piano bows her head
to look down the cracks between the keys,

their bone shattered into a little music
that says, I know, pain is solitary,

your talk of it more solitary still,
but even that has a tune inside it,

and inside that a cadence, a silence
so deep, embedded in the measures,

you hear the sounds of others there.
A cough, a cry, a train in the distance.

Which is when the woman lifts her hands
startled by the music no music makes,

the broken pair of glasses it discovers
after the dust has tumbled to the street.

Under every street she hears another,
and still the keys move a while longer,

pulled, it would seem, from strings below,
like a debt that is always left

to settle, a call to the thing she did
not suffer, see, or ever mean to say.

Jon Faddis and the High Note

Hard to look, harder still to look away,
to brush aside the brutal accident
that was his smile, the writhe of the incisor,
the gap you could slip a house key through.

So, sure, the other children mocked him,
though he too pushed forward, unaware
of the music here, in the wretched little
puzzle of his mouth, its pieces missing.

Or so it seemed until the year he pressed
a trumpet to his lips, his narrow embouchure
developing in time the highest spirits
of his range, far beyond the reach of others.

Notes flew from his battered instrument
like a light-beam bearing a lonely movie,
a story drawn through the bar room smoke,
over the clink and laughter of the tables.

To pierce the night sky that way, it took
more than the ferocity of pride,
the spit that gathered in its coil and valve,
more than hurricanes in a pin of air.

You could hear the brass sweeten in him,
as if there were angels on that pin,
as if the arrows of his straight tones
wavered in their feathers as they struck.

The walls that wore his face, they revealed
only so much, like any tune, his lips
smothered with his trumpet, or simply closed
as he looked back, more dire than his songs.

If you knew him then, you knew the rest,
how he paid to have his teeth fixed and lost
three octaves, then returned at crack of day
to have the gap restored. It was the way

he entered music, through the great disorder,
the shame even, the birthright he covered up,
as if some necessary dark kicked
to send him back, reeling into music.

You see it in the tortured look, not only
of his teeth, but of anyone who lifts a lot
of wind into the atmosphere, cheeks flushed,
because, truth is, it takes more blood, more

luster, the higher you go. It takes years
in the smolder and stench of rooms, broken
or unbroken a bite beneath the pressed flesh,
a wing in the pitch of the upturned horn.

Hendrix

And in those final moments as he played
with fire, remember the thread he poured,
clear as music, over his paisley Strat.
Remember how he knelt to coax the static:
a stunt, he would admit, and it worked,
the way fire works to make us talk.
It destroyed a perfectly good guitar,
the kind boys covet, to lead us, where?
Into spectacle, smoke, less than smoke?
The genius of the young is how they grow
younger as we age. The day the sun
devours the earth, history is no heaven.
More of a film lodged in its projector.
Just like fire to eat the memory of fire,
the body drowned in wine the morning after.
If it's true, that death is a mother,
if all we own begins where it ends,
in silence, which is the greater flame, the thing
that embodied us, or the song it sings?

Acolyte

To unlock the neck of an old guitar,
it takes a little warmth, not enough
to crack it, mind you, just a touch here
and there, enough to drug the glue, if

it's animal glue, the sap that weeps
inside the body of the instrument.
Which is why they use a lamp to heat
the seam, to lower the relief, the light

like oil in the tumblers of a door.
It takes a sun's patience, true, the kind
that liquefies the sleeper as he stares
up from sleep. To move is to mend,

to coax the slow structure of the wood
like a book we cradle, a broken spine.
To make the mind matter, matter mind,
it is the dream of things. Every song

we close our eyes to play, the glad noise
of our farewells, it plants a seed, a spark
inside the mouth, the cup, the wine we raise,
the blood that pries us open as we drink.

Elegy for a Coffin in the Shape of a Guitar

There are sicknesses that cure the sick.
Why else do people smile as they crawl
into your cabinet which is, after all,
a place that shudders with a kind of music.

The body, we call it, your figure almost human,
a thing made curvaceous as a question,
full of the tremors of revival, but then
again, a little bit dead. Think of heaven,

how the more we age, the more we fret,
the more a body withers into bloom.
That's how it is with tone-wood. In time
the sound hole ripens to a great black fruit.

Granted, yours is painted there, but open
to suggestion. What do you expect,
that you would lead us to the spectacle.
Better to be our last, our best illusion,

as if the fetishes we love to death
grow monstrous with our love and eat us.
Silly, the way that monsters are, the lust
that overtakes the instruments of flesh,

the bewildered lust that makes us young.
And so we give you to the earth, to sing
the planet into circles, like skirts that fling
inside some childhood memory of song.

We entrust you not to the autumn leaves
but to something less material,
to the music enveloping a cradle
or a grave, the final make-believe

of what we bend our knees to hear. We love
you like a rhythm that fades inside us,
our eyes closed beneath the maples, the fist
that is the heart we swallow, buried alive.

Tympanum

Phantom voices, you called them
as a boy, just a year
from the fever that left you
deaf, a child of the child
you were, of the one
whose history, however brief,
filled in the sounds
where silence made them.
Phantom as in *phantom limb*,
so long, that is, as you watched
her lips, the way they healed
and opened as she spoke.
And though you knew it
as a lie, this sound, you swore
by everything you heard
the source was out there,
like a god who searched
the night for one believer.
And yes, the stuff between
her lips was darkness
mostly, but when you watched
the parting of the flesh
that gave you words, it's dusk
you thought of, the wing beat
of your native colors.
Each voice a conversation.
A prayer. A *hello* you lowered
into a well that echoed back,
inquiring. Who was anyone
to tell you where it started,
this language that made

its maker, that never ceased
to surprise, the visual
music a mother still, save
when she turned her face to see
what a child sees.

Homage to Sebastian Stenzel

After the cedar died in the great fire,
it stood for eighty years. A testament
to what the long neglected can endure
if the roots go deep, the heartwood dense,
grain woven, limbs upholding nothing
like a nervous system of the sky.

No need to clear the lion's share of damage,
the land the blaze blackened for a season,
though naturally they razed the crumpled home.
What the fire began, men completed,
and there were those who were buried here
and there, and those who never reappeared.

What remained was the flame of soot
that climbed the tower, our useless miracle,
guardian of those who stood in its shadows
and suffered without record, passing through
the stories and nightmares of a few
friends, neighbors, until they too passed on.

Nights, the long and stubborn musculature
swung its axe in the wind, laying low
a silence in the branches, and in the stars
that slept there, that burned for eighty years.
It took a luthier to bring them down,
to see in the tone-wood a slow growth

the winters made stiff and tight, ideal
in its resistance and yield, its open voice.
So yes, he destroyed it, quarter sawn so
the monument might fall again, and again,
over and over as song in the startled
braces of the instrument. Or so he hoped.

It takes a little faith to flex the final
cut, to tap it, listening for some pitch
to draw breath in the unspoken, to say
I am out there somewhere, as music is
in the reticence of things. It takes
an ember's patience to plane the wood just so,

to fit it over the casket, over the memory
of one note dying into the next,
into some solitary conversation,
the still bodies of those who listen, those
who, for the moment they are listening,
stand in the fire, made tall, and have no name.

EARTH'S APPRENTICE

Then he cast aside his shovel and asked
the pit, if each instant is a still place,
and the day ahead is made of them,
how is it the heart's arrow ever moves.
And the hole said nothing. He waited,
it waited, and in the silent space
he smelled something of the earth going
through him, without mercy, malice, or end.

I.

The Cutting of Flowers

for Alan Watts

1. Crown

Is it true, we are born not into the world,
but out of it, the crown of our experience

pulled through some tear in the fabric.
From the world to what, we cannot say,

only that we break open our eyes,
our mouths, that we cry to breathe,

and on it goes, flower after flower
drawn through the cup of the one before.

So if we arrive, flush with confusion,
our native tongue, can you blame us,

given over to the giants that speak our name.
The self is out there, somewhere,

not the world, but what it harbors,
the emptiness a mother leaves when she leaves the room.

The flower knows. From this to that, and beyond that
the sun that scorches the stalk into a fruit.

Eat, says the world. I am no one's
if not yours now, cut to bloody the hand I feed.

2. Branch

To pound the hammer, it takes a fist.
It takes an axis in our grip,

a hole in the body where the power goes.
It takes the force of human foresight

to close our space, to make of it
a box of windows, the breakable parts

where the sky pours in. Suns fall.
Bicycles crackle through the leaves and chime.

We love how the quiet light crashes into things.
For beyond a home we need a world

to house it, and strength enough to lift our heads
the way my father lifted a family tree,

with branches to vein the blue behind it.
Somewhere above ground, he hammered a floor

where I could stand, tall as the father
I was not, in fact, would never be,

just a son, a boy in the design, fleshed
in leaves, a nail buried in the hand of autumn.

3. Root

This world, this tangle of nerves and veins,
what is it if not the grip of a root that feeds the flower.

How many times I took the soil for the sky,
the sky for the heaven, the nightfall for the thing unknown.

If love wears the face of dread, it too is a blossom,
what triggers the cries of birds from the branches.

These days the entire garden sings on its hinges.
The body, I say, though I am thinking of yours,

the surgeon's scar the seam of a new emptiness,
the root gone though a stem remains.

It is the color of emergency, of the blaze
it runs to, the shattered vessel of the eye.

It is every hope, every stem that opens, breaking,
faithfully, without regret, cut and gathered

into a gift, a promise, a convalescence, a whole
roomful of gifts. As if it were still there, the root,

a thousand roots, all of them groping in the great
dark of missing things, aching into bloom.

4. Follow

My mother's journey was a nail
that drove always in one direction,

deeper into the hard part, until the day
it stopped, complete, fully seated in the darkness.

Pain is pain, I do not doubt that,
but more than this, she argued bitterly with time

to turn back, as if every throb
was the bell of some cathedral, some message

sent out to a sky that never responded.
One direction, like the face we live in,

the one we push ahead to shield us from the blows.
All her life she prepared for a season she knew

so little about, where she would wander
late and listen to the clocks, where they chipped the huge

rock of silence. Whatever it was the chimes said,
it was obsolete the moment that they said it.

A body moves, and we follow. Like it or not,
she follows me still. This is what it means to obey.

5. Pledge

What did we mean, hand over heart,
when we said those words, flesh

on flesh, to lay a shield over the place
that we in turn laid bare, the bewildered

muscle writhing in the dark.
And to the country for witches stand,

I said, anything to please, to play my part.
And as we chanted, our flag in its bracket

high above the map of the world,
whatever allegiance I could muster was confused

with opposition, the kind that plays chicken,
or breaks the tape at the Olympics.

It's a free country, we said when we were mean.
Under God, our king, and no less distant,

like the dad I mistook in the market
for mine, the one who turned to look down,

surprised, with a smile that scared me
speechless, my hand a stranger fastened to his coat.

6. Ice

When my father died, I inherited his ring,
its eye looking back at all I did and did not do.

If only I could fill it, and so belong,
though I never could, nor could he those final days

he wasted to the bone the ring would slip from.
And though the circle broke for no one,

neither did the zero that gripped him
the way my mother did, my father in his Navy

whites, his bewildered body returned
from a sea of things they never spoke of.

Marriage is made of such things, and understands
what goes unsaid creates a space

that waits for one to break the ice.
Sometimes my father hardly let me speak,

neck-deep in words, save when he lost them
in the end, when he looked up and waited,

his garbled sounds repeated by me as questions,
and he gestured simply, as fathers do, yes or no, yes or no.

7. Winter

So tempting, to read into your palm
the fate that carves a body as you age.

The line drawn down your wrist,
you see it as one more shadow

pulled among the shadows at dusk
until it bleeds into the others.

But a hand knows no more than it did,
slipped beneath your pillow,

cupped to catch the face above it.
What happens happens slow,

each palm a pane of glass shattered by the sun.
Or better yet, a guitar, its finish

crazed by time. Its prophesies
are music, which is to say

neither true nor false.
What did we expect, a lesser instrument,

or something more seasoned, alive,
that shudders with a prospect it cannot hold.

8. Bridal

When the mind says to the body, it's time,
and lo, the body begins to rise,

what language does it use.
Does the flesh look back, puzzled as an animal.

Or is the body one more tongue
a spirit speaks, surprised a little,

as language is, by what it has to say.
How do I look, the bride says to the mirror,

and the mirror replies, you tell me,
and the bride says, what are you, my therapist,

and it goes on that way, until darkness falls
into the glass and sweeps her figure through.

One rope, one life, to have, to hold.
So the bride says to the groom, imagine

I am the bell and you the tongue— or is it the other way—
do you feel it too, this cry to the distance.

And before he can manage a word,
her body—or is it his—chimes in: I do, I do.

9. Shine

Then the verbs ran their sparklers along the waterfront,
racing the current they mirrored into,

working up to the speed of the world,
however hopeless, for soon they would run out

of breath, as words will, and slow down inside
the chirps of frogs charming the reeds.

Flies swooned over the water.
A green stain of pollen ribboned the shine.

And for a moment the minds of the verbs
greened with pollen, or so they swore to murky places

beneath the shine, to a stillness in the idea
of stillness, as if stillness were a verb.

And the shine rose and fell to the rhythm
of the clouds, the great sky-clock pulsing sleepily,

dipping in and out of the current. The frogs too
were charmed, panting, silent, bubbling the shallows,

a listening song in their fearful hiding,
in the tiny misshapen hearts of the verbs.

10. Reincarnation

So we were driving into the woods of words
until they blackened the stars and we were all

eyes and blind, no body to get us out
of the place. My world, such big ideas we had.

Which is how the future made near sense to me,
the big idea like a giant meatloaf at the end

of history. So we were driving into words,
eager for a dignified cheese to get lost in,

a chrome diner gleaming in the forest.
But I was younger than I thought I would have been,

when we were all aging in the big idea together,
each at the oracle of her amen, a turkey

printing its roasted scent on the air. Hmmm.
Smell that final earthling on its axis.

And it was something we would eat together
in the way you eat when you're not even hungry,

just the pure anxiety at the end of desire
driving you back into the body of the bird.

11. Dirt

As a boy, I took comfort in it, wore it, ate it,
cracked it with a spade and thought

some day I would make it clear to Asia,
soiled with wounds that were a heart's

way of breaking to the surface.
If my mother called out in worry, no matter.

I just went a little farther, her voice
lost to those of missiles in my mouth.

Make yourself small, said my teacher
during drop drills in our class, and we snapped

beneath our desks, fetal, blind, digging in.
Tough to dig, for a kid my size, and I imagined

men with boots on the hilts of shovels.
Their graves. For what do the dead own,

really, save a passing thought now and then.
Or a shy place in a mother's voice,

my roof a dusk, my name a question,
as she calls into the deepening sky.

12. Eden

The thing that has not happened yet,
it lies far behind you, in the mainsprings

of gardens that blossom in the past.
The sound of clockwork walks across your room,

over your face where you lie still to recall
something so distant you need

to make it simple. You need to forget.
Claire, if you are listening, I can only imagine

what it is to lie in the field
of a childhood that darkens to accept you.

The fertile gardens are old. I know.
When you look up this evening at your child,

my wife, the orphan mother of no one now,
is it the future that looks back, its thread

drawn through the needle of your eye.
What gift is this to the girl buried in your body,

and in your mother's before that, and so on.
In every flower, a mouth, a breath, the parting of the womb.

II.

Earth's Apprentice

1. Salt

If this is where our chronicle began,
in the grit of an ocean as it conceived
the sprouts of legs we crawled ashore on;
if the grains we bore became the seed

so quick to clarify, to raise the phantom
voice that lifts our story from its page;
if as we read our eyes begin to swim,
even as they hover, to take the plunge

over and over, immersed in the thing
they cannot see; if small lives burn inside
the wound, inside the throat we sting
with salt to wash away the parasite;

is it any wonder, the blind memory
in all we keep close, in what preserves
our sight, our skin, the dark shade and mercy
of our meat, the sobbing of the waves.

2. Amber

Just when in any story does a wave
become a wave. Amber is no stone,
but life's current pulled beyond our lives,
crushed beneath the ocean like a sun.

Elegiac, the way it holds the flame
of things, however small, the wing, the stem,
the shell in its resin, time's perfume
a ghost, slow to vaporize the tomb.

Centuries have given us the harp
shade you find in a large print book
of angels, or buried in the cold sap
that wept against the floor of the Baltic.

Ask the widow if the blood is deep
enough to drown in. Like a man's eye
that awakens after months of sleep,
her face in the lens a stranger, a fly.

3. Limestone

Our law was built to withstand the wind,
here where spring is no paradise, strong
against the courthouse tower, our stones bound
in grit, chiseled thick as an arm is long.

And at the entrance a Confederate
soldier, a boy—he too is chiseled—his face
a tomb of old confusions, of nights
he woke, panicked by his father's voice.

Mostly he goes unnoticed, oblivious
in turn, where the hammers rise and fall
against the criminal. The last bar closes.
Some child writes his hatred on the wall.

It's everywhere and nowhere, like blood.
Or nails no nation sinks beneath its gavel.
Only time. The other fatherhood.
Stones without the conscience to be cruel.

4. Flint

A man blows a mindful little prayer
over his plate of meat, less in guilt,
he tells you, than gratitude, a bit of air
to season the sacrament, like a ghost.

He is no killer, and so a killer's visions,
in the distance those who make the hunt
a rite, what begins where hunger begins
to chip its arrowhead, to bind the flint.

A gift, to sharpen as you break, winged
with edges to lodge inside the animal,
to travel one direction, the suffering
slowly draining from your act, your kill.

Wind was made for occasions like this,
to carry the scent like a thing on a fork
into a mouth inside the wilderness,
in every cell a stone, a hammer, a spark.

5. Radium

Light is a river, and all that radiates
a stream inside the river. Ask any rock
when it glows, solvent in the current
of its shine. Ask the blue hands of clocks

as they too would glow. Or the women
who once painted these dials with radium,
mute as they licked their brushes to sharpen
their aim, a spark of blue against each tongue.

One hopeful even did her nails with it.
Blue the eye, and bluer still the man
inside the eye. Leave it to the bright
to break into the facets of the diamond.

It would open most anything, a stem,
a particle, a bone, a city. Somewhere
a woman looks up to read the time,
and, forever dark, time returns the favor.

6. Garnet

The boy king whose face we see done
in gold, did he pose in life, in fear
perhaps, as the sculptor crowned the sun
of his head, his glass complexion far

too young, it seems, for the braided column
of his beard, his eyes wide though glazed
with a certain steadiness, a calm
unlike a child's, let alone one faced

with his journey into the underworld.
Is this his own resolve or the mask
his power gave him to wear, to uphold
like a man trapped in the obelisk

of his own myth. Did the afterlife
weigh his soul as if it were the art
he loved, even as he turned to cough
blood, his human blood, bright as garnet.

7. Cobalt

The acetylene torch of elements,
a shade so cold it burns, the color of skies
that illuminate the cathedral print
in a Book of Hours, in a Gemini

scene that pours the welder's blue of heaven
(the chaste blue that polishes the sun)
over the roofs below, over everyone's
scarf and mantle, the robe of the man

who swings his scythe, or the peasant dress
of women who gather clippings into rows.
Backs bend beneath the cobalt paradise
of cloth, of star, of paper. So many echoes

among them, there must be an emptiness
somewhere, a depth beyond the parapets
where the sky of the poor, the nameless
ploughman, ignites the earth he shall inherit.

8. Quicksilver

For the insatiable Flamel it meant
the secret to the philosopher's stone,
which is why he slipped the element
back and forth, trickled the tiny suns

from hand to hand, too innocent to know
the everlasting life that he looked for
deep inside his melancholia slowly
poisoned him, dizzied him with quicksilver.

Perhaps you see it in a child's puzzle
you cannot master, you cannot put away,
a maze filled with the watery metal.
Temperamental. Like the fever of days

that rise and fall in our thermometers.
We too rise and fall, into beds, the cold,
the pills we take, the need for always more
to cure us, to turn the body into gold.

9. Marble

Five hours into flight, the Apollo threw
back to earth an image of the world
as the island we all know, the blue
marble, this speculum, this toy, the swirled

uncertainties of weather circumscribed,
the kind of symmetry of accidents
you see in living things, the human eye,
its craze of tiny pigments beneath lens.

Cast out of nature's circle like a watch-
maker god, more foreign than divine,
we feel a lonely power, its surge, its crutch,
as if our rocket came this far to divide

and conquer, to dwindle our seas, the milk
of ice. Even our bodies become weightless,
raised up from the defilement, the muck
that made us, the whole damn thing that rolls away.

10. Chalk

Minutes just before the tip, the power
forward powders his hands, tosses a fist
of dust into the air, a thing to master
the law of falling bodies, while they last.

Even ghosts have anatomy that dies
with us, like the pictures children leave
against the sidewalk, the clouds of paradise
pale with the skeletons chalk is made of.

Soon our drawing sticks grind down to stones
of nearly nothing, down to the bone, our bone.
The star player throws up a prayer. Soon
the night ahead grows hard enough to write on.

And yes, we love our bodies, which is why
we fear them, leave them even, why children
make their mark, their figures in the sky
we travel. And then the falling of the rain.

11. Carbon

In every shroud you find a trace of it,
the carbon of the air we all inhale,
its ghost a date woven in the fabric
of things, the mind of the material.

So when they laid out the burial cloth
to map the face of god, it looked up,
or rather the face inside the face, the death
of death in the object of their worship.

It takes a bowed head to examine what
a head alone cannot, to bear witness
like an eye that turns back in its socket
to see itself inside the wilderness.

Ask carbon. To see is not to believe
a hoax, but to allow the miraculous
light that gave mere man his century,
and ours, to burn god's image into us.

12. Sand

So many grains, so many little tombs
of dust. It keeps us humble: the deceased,
always slightly larger than their time,
larger than us, no less, just as a breeze

is larger than the cloud that blows it. More
stars in the sky than granules on the shore.
I believe that, as I believe no one here
would count it out, counting on it rather

the way the sand counts on gravity
to pull it, to drain the thread, its current
to the earth. So many grains, so many
friends now gone the way of the moment,

of the age that bore them, the one they bore.
Which is to see our past as large, blessed
to have such giants in it, such wind to bear
their loss, to stretch our sails like blown glass.

III.

Wildlife Studies

1. Nest

Begin with a thread, however small,
the kind the ash-throated flycatcher weaves
into a nest, a fury, a bristle of sticks

and little throats, the makeshift crosshatch
of all the brittle wreckage of the yard:
the cigarette filter, bits of string,

skeletal leaves in the shapes of trees.
Somewhere a lace slips through an eyelet.
A snake skin rises from the leaves.

Some break in the weather calls all birds
to stitch the illegible into a new order,
which in turn longs to raise a little hell.

To weave not only the eye of the nest
but the hunger that fills it, the lantern
made of feathers that spill over into light.

A cradle of music then, like the open
wound of a trumpet that plays so sweet
the men of both garrisons stop to listen.

And what a soldier hears is what we all hear,
the new dead come to life, if only briefly,
staring up in their blindness at the stars.

Wind blows the brittle grass of their hair.
They too are made of hollow places, nests,
their mouths gaping, calling out in song.

2. Tusk

The pianist lays her fingers across the bone
white keys, against the harvested teeth
of the great pacific beast that once raised

a cry between them, unhurried as he paused,
deep in thought, or the cracks in thought,
then knelt to fill his trumpet at the stream.

Just where the roar began is a mystery,
a throat sunk at the bottom of his throat.
Listen as the magnum takes him down,

as he buckles beneath the heft of all
that beauty. What does an elephant care
that his body fractures into octaves.

In truth, his ivory is less the soul
you hear than the armature around it.
Tusk or no tusk, music is a pulse

beneath the hand that would make it useful,
a place so vast we measure it in time.
In this way, it carries what we cannot.

Phrases expand, contract, and it is their
fading that bears the heart along. These strings,
they can shoulder thirty tons of tension.

A lot, says the body. Which is true.
And the soul responds with the lightest
touch, a pale chord that dies to crush us.

3. Siren

Here where the city meets the kindling
of the foothills, it takes so little to raise
a hidden voice, to set the dark on fire.

An ambulance splits the dotted line.
It must go somewhere, god knows, and we
who lie awake hear it echo in the wild.

I read once that coyotes howl to say,
I am here, my friends, come and find me.
Or was it, I am here, rivals, stay away.

Even the domestic among us feel
a star come down as they lift their throats.
Their eyes close in the waking pleasure

of sleep, what braids their voices into one.
When I was a boy, I woke to this cry
as it traveled from yard to yard, and saw

the medics storm a door across the street.
The only house with its lights still burning.
I swore I heard a woman break down,

or some animal, I was not sure.
Was it song or anguish in the sirens
of dogs as they faded into night.

Then came sleep, and the traffic mended.
I am here, said the heart, just barely,
or this: I am everywhere, stay away.

4. Seize

Clouds obscure the moon and so light up
my name for moon. Most of what I know
arrives unseen, screened, as the blush

that illuminates my world wide web,
my liquid crystal as it friends the dark.
I was born with a moon-shaped hole

in my eye, the O of the eclipse,
moon of the other side of the moon.
Each night I see a cloud of ink, the sea

creature in panic, her signature flown
in the flourish of her disappearance.
All those arms, those weeds in the current,

each with its own mind, its own confusion.
The color black gets larger on the inside.
Which is what a brain is after all,

or the monitor I surf for words.
When I turn to the world at my desk,
the computer, the calendar, the phone,

I see the many arms of an octopus,
how solitary the woven branches.
When its cavity convulses it propels.

I love that. The way I love the word *cast:*
thrown forward and thus incarnate. Dear word
with your arms of ink. Are you listening.

5. Volition

The bee that gems my cup is no stranger
to a little chaos, the honey on the wind,
the ghost of a choice in the world design.

The beads of head, thorax, and abdomen
grip the string that buzzes as it flies.
Therefore the music that we call a bee.

Compelled, which says a bee is two bees,
one a bloom to animate the other.
He tilts his head, polishes the sweetened

hairs of his antennae, his shell a shelter
anonymous with guests we cannot see.
Is it true, each being is a reader,

not bees alone, but the buds they open
peeled to read the hunter reading them.
It makes him lovable and dangerous,

the unscripted molecule of bee
a scribble among flowers, crazy with rain.
Take this mandible, this tiny nib

that pins the air, pauses, pins again.
No form without no form, it writes. OK.
So I made that up. It goes more like this:

once I was a bee inside a bee.
Or this: mind is the only wilderness,
a rose torn from hiding, like a sting.

6. Shell

Water knows. If you pour a man
into a chair, he becomes the chair
for some smaller man, or chair, his shape

the shape of what he's in and so is not.
You could easily fall asleep in these arms,
a star inside the waters where you drown.

There is always tomorrow, says the turtle,
who closes her eyes like the part in the dream
that no longer dreams, when all goes dark.

A turtle knows. It takes a little distance
to be a river, a little give, to sleep
the sleep of the man anxious for his

blood work, who drifts off in spite of all.
This is what it is to be both dweller
and the dwelling. When I talk to others

who count down the minutes, I am always
talking to some comrade from afar.
Myself, for one, just one among many

who step away from me into the heartbreak.
We know a turtle suffers, because who doesn't,
in spite of armor, in light of it, the living

stone. Inside a river you find a river.
Inside a turtle, well, please don't. And deep
inside the looking glass, a shattering of birds.

7. Crossfire

When a woodcock flushes from a thicket,
the sky he enters is two skies, his eyes
set so far back he sees in wide angles

both horizons, camouflaged in light.
Just the slightest break in the circle
of his vision, or is it two visions,

with one tremor of vigilance between them.
Who are we to know. We whose eyes
inhale a spirit through the crossfire,

through the singular iris of the mind.
A whisper pulls the trigger on his wings.
Does he know the bright circumference

is broken by a blindness at his back,
a danger, yes, and so a center, an iron
wedge in the fire of the visual.

Always the ache of the invisible,
the will to survive thrust among the pieces.
The woodcock tilts his head, the world a puzzle

so large in him his brain sits upside down
the way a sky sits in the eyes of lakes.
When he stares ahead into a future,

it looks right through him. When he is hit,
it is one voice, one animal that cries
to break the pool of heaven where he falls.

8. Energeia

So difficult to think with this fly
that ticks timelessly against the glass,
against a day we call the day ahead.

Poor fly. Then again, what do I know
of a fly's joy, the sizzle of its task,
the tension in the clockwork of things.

Everywhere you look, you see inside
the dead the not yet dead, the rivulet
of black stars that trickle to the earth.

Are we not watchman, all of us flies.
I read a man once who says the more
precisely you measure the location

of a particle the less you know
of its momentum. He was sure of it,
the way we are sure a day will come

to flood the eyes of ponds and houses.
Which is worse: a fear of what you know
or what you don't. These nights a shadowy

bluster of elms plunges like a ship.
Can you blame the world if it moves
one half against another. The pebble we balance

on a grave we visit, it pins us to it
as it melts. It belongs. Here, or somewhere.
The closer we get the more it disappears.

9. Camouflage

The man with the transparent eyeball
is nothing. Or so he would have it, to see all,
which is to say all things in the distance,

to welcome back the objects in the room
through a lens of distance, like an old friend
you meet at an old friend's funeral.

Granted, we are children, and so too big
for our bodies, too small for the sky
that aches inside us as it fades to black.

Ask the lizard if he blushes green
to hide from a world by becoming it,
by wearing a little jacket made of leaves.

They redden. He reddens. They tremble,
and you can just make out a little fear
in the starless regions of his gaze.

The man with the eye is not alone.
He too walks home with thoughts to lay them
down on paper, to name his friends again.

Beyond that, these words that fall like skins
over man and lizard, they are less
opaque now, in light of the journey.

And as he stares outside in search of them,
he might be looking at a tiny heartbeat,
green with a season he cannot see is there.

10. Night Arrival

My eyes read my eyelids when I dream
the long straight ache of miles below.
It's exhausting, the great chain of being

alive, bed to the floor, floor to the planet.
The heart beats its pillow like a path.
Some nights I walk forever that way,

unsure of what it is I walk, if what
they say is true, that the world as we know it
stands on the back of an elephant

who stands on a turtle, and under him
another, and so on down the endless stairs.
What is it that speaks before it speaks.

That thing you cannot find the words for,
it falls away the moment that you find them.
Some days you hear it singing as it falls.

What does it explain if I believe
language is the mother of its language.
Every voice a child, a little stranger,

born of flesh and the hole inside it.
If you holler in this well, you hear
it reply in the form of a question.

The limits of my language are the beginnings
of my world. *Wait and see*, says the world.
And see, and see, the tunnel of the eye.

Audubon

1.

The night my father died I buried myself
in a little language, a testament of will,
measured out the way the stonecutter

measures out our names to make them fit,
and as I leaned beneath the bell of light
to the cursor where it pulsed, I placed there

neither man nor the shape of his absence,
not grief as I knew it, but the tiny bones
of ink that grief made, rising to the surface.

I have met with those who disapprove
of passing through too quickly into song,
as if, with death, we give to it the first

word which is none at all. Anything more
is to make light of suffering: mine, yours.
Or worse, to make far too much of it,

to lose oneself in the futures market
that seeks to clear a profit on misfortune.
They have a point. That is, some songs need

a certain hesitation to break the ice
and move more deeply into winter's current.
Then again, tending to a song's needs

gives loss a vocation, and who is to say
what will come of it, any more
than what comes of music while it lasts.

2.

Audubon loved the creatures that he killed.
That is part of the story. He loved the music
he silenced, gutted, stuffed with clouds of cotton,

the bodies he cleansed with a surgeon's care
then mended with needle, a stitched seam
tucked beneath the feathers where they shone.

He loved the eyes that gave way to seeds
of glass, the small black blisters gleaming
with light that went just so far, so deep.

Somewhere in that region of inquiry,
in what he could not paint, the illusion
of life took, and fluttered to the surface,

informing the angle of the head, the beak,
the bright rustle of wings as the ivory-
billed woodpecker turns away from us

to make out some motion in the distance.
Movement is danger. Or so the heartbeat
says at first, until it settles back

onto its perch, its branch of understanding.
What you see within the sure lines and blush
of these renditions is an artist's gaze,

so steady, cautious as it crosses the lip
of stillness, our open coffin, careful not
to break the perfect silence where it breathes.

3.

Suppose all the world is a house lit up
against the night, and the eye of the bird
our only window. If you look through

the black air, you just might see a man,
a father, say, who takes his broken sleep
down the hall to a desk in the distance.

He is peering over his heavy glasses
to the near at hand, papers that await
his signature to put his affairs in order.

When he writes, his pen bleeds a little
ink over the line, real or imagined,
to lay a name against the emptiness.

Birds slip into the flowered portraits
of his study, silent, and yet made flesh
by the hand that murdered to create them.

The Carolina pigeon dips the nib
of his beak into the mouth he feeds.
If he spreads his colors, ribbed in black,

it is one more song that calls the thing
unseen. The man closes up his desk,
and with it a passage in his testament,

the part where he asks to be scattered,
remembered the way a body remembers to breathe.
A ghost thread pulls outward, like a word.

HOMAGE TO PHOSPHORUS

And so it came, the water, and as it rose
and the man leaned a little closer
to see what night had left there,
his stare became a hole in the surface,
as if that were what a man is, what
a world is not, so says the hole, the ice
of the mirror he shatters as he drinks.

I.

Homage to Phosphorus

Phos, light, *pherein*, to bear, and bear it
we must, as the compounds of the brain
will tell you, there is no thought without it.

True, there are horrors in this story,
the napalm that drenched the boy who ran barefoot
toward the camera, his arms opened slightly

so as not to sting himself with himself.
And before that, the bones of women
brittle with the stuff it took to work

the match factories of the past. Proof.
The molecules of fire will kill you.
Which is more than the man could know,

the alchemist who stumbled on it first
in his search for the philosopher's stone,
his hands scarred with alkali and acid.

His eyes poor, head bowed, he raised a puzzle
of glass to corrupt things and so make them
pure, to steam the urine in his flask.

Which is when a snow began to fall
like nights we are sleeping and the dust
that burns white with cold gathers below.

As a boy I owned a toy moon that glowed
with something toxic on the one side,
and I inhaled its sulfurous smell, thinking

I too would drink the shine of the place
and give it back to darkness. In reality
phosphorescence was no mirror, no moon,

but a furnace that consumes the air.
Those were the years of the rain and war
in southeast Asia. I barely understood it,

even though the cameras offered us
the parts a nation could not take, and did.
Somewhere great blooms of phosphorus fell

from crop dusters and crinkled through the vines.
Mostly those who volunteered were boys.
And neither old nor brave enough, I killed

my toys of them, green beneath a moon
that had two sides, one dead, the other deadly.
One disaster led to another, to the cross-

hair flash that was death from a distance.
The new wars look less and less like wars.
Just a snow of little conflagrations

that break against the desert in the night.
History does not repeat itself. It burns
a map across the child, a country that spreads

into an empire I do not recognize
as mine. It burns the way gold burns,
or the sun that would liquefy our gold,

or the sickness that lingers long after
some difficult fact, some news, say,
made strange and personal by a soldier

at the door in dress blues; one word and she
who receives it suddenly a widow,
transfixed by fire, her eye wet with new light.

Tropical

From the Greek *tropos,* to turn,
as in the turning of a sphere,
the arc of the passage the sun
blazes, straying just so far

from our equator, turning back
at the Tropics of Capricorn
and Cancer, each winter wake
of stars abandoned, frozen, scorned.

Tropos, as in *phototropic,*
the way the sun's fire drags
across the gardenia, the fig,
the scorched eyes of the island grasses.

We could waste away dazed
on the savannah, forever ripe
with obscenities of paradise,
the gash of summer fruit. *To trope,*

to rout, and thus our *trophy,* minted
in the blood of those we honor.
Remember. The graven monument
that turns away the face of horror.

And whose trophy is it, whose peace,
when we kneel to read the word's
eroded tablet, whose one place
drowned in a threnody of birds.

Imagine the tongue that tropes, the kind
that bends the metal of our reason
to some buried will, to the mind's
dark, its welter, its grief, its treason

However strong the twist, the turn
in the long order of things, is it
any less the figure a surgeon
makes, the brightened seam he cuts;

any less the *trope*, the final
gush of *alleluias*, like a sin
turned to faith, or a sun's refusal
tearing down the blind horizon.

Map

No, it did not bring us here.
Nor does it lead us from the squalor.
All we can make of the map
is how it testifies to where
we've been, streets that fire up
behind us, the abandoned beds
of men and rivers, sunset strips
blind to all but straight ahead.
Such is the arrow of our days,
to live forward, know in reverse,
to draw back shade after shade
of smoke, led behind the force
that splits these mountains into towns.
Our planet is the kind of dream
a fact dreams, the undertow
of some extinction still unseen
inside the shifting land, the slow
sure acid waters, cliffs of ice
that break and shudder from their grip.
Against the anger of the tides
that clack our sails, we send our ships
into no man's future and wait.
And though a fisted wind strips
the power from our homes, to break
our stride, our faith, our picture window,
we sleep it off, too soon returned
not to where we live, but how,
here as the stars come out to burn,
a map on fire inside our lantern.

The Remorse of Narcissus

It feels older, blinder, this April fog,
older than the ground it rises out of
everywhere, it seems, or no one place,

as if all of morning covered up its ears
to listen. Self, I say, you may not know me.
I am the keeper of the name you bear

into the plain speech of difficult hours.
I am the kindling of hands beneath you
as you sleep, the death-bed words too small

to whisper. I am smoke. I see that now.
I see time as a coin I never give, take,
return at last, flashing in a pool of coins.

To ask more is to ask forgiveness. I ask
forgiveness. I am the child lost in traffic,
the leaden brood of the anvil cloud

dragging a shadow of sirens into day.
I am the bridge that burns its way to see.
Tell me, self, where is your mentor now,

where the gentle smolder of his beard.
Where the spontaneity of wings
that weave a veil about the steeple.

I would walk into death and back for you.
I would eat my bitterness like a starved dream.
I would call out to the father buried

inside you, tell him I am trying, always,
the roof of my house in shambles, a storm
of needles crackling at my window. Self,

I say, come into the sphere by the fire,
take off your gloves. There's more of the world
than sky to hold it, more ebb and flow

than a shore can bear. And the self turns
around to say what any echoing canyon
says, any vast, hard, and empty place.

Graviton

In Memory of John Ciardi

The star you see is no star,
but the satellite that steers

this town, tied as it is to a seed
of light with a clock inside.

Ask any angel. It knows
with gravity the heartbeat slows.

A man sleeps. An apple falls.
And still it's inexplicable.

Of all the atom's particles,
the graviton gives us so little:

just an error in the equation,
a thing gone missing, like a man.

Once I opened a letter late,
just after the one who wrote it

died. That was long ago, Denver,
the winter of '86, and never

had we suffered a heavier snow.
Cars passed out in gutters. Trees broke.

Our pupils contracted in the sun.
Our home was so much smaller then.

Somewhere in the distance, a bell
struck one and so pierced a hole

in the quiet. Almost still.
And then the scraping of the shovels.

Homage to Lead

Not the melancholic bottom of the well,
the cloud-slate of the murky surface,
the shrouded moon, the unraveled bed.

No defeated pallor. No head in hand
impatient for the storm to pass right through.
Not fated in the way of the fat calf

who lumbers off to the moaning shelter,
or the widow veil of the miner's lung.
Impure, demonic, the still born child.

No, it is another lead I want to praise.
the thing that centers the pans of the balance,
or cuts the tiny zero at the crux.

So self-assured in the open palm.
Let water be subtle and swift. Let it run
through the hour like a thread of sand.

But lead has the quiet engraver's hand
that lays its nocturne on the fray. Lead
as the thing that writes, the thing that's written,

the string that leads us from the labyrinth.
It's the part we did not know we know.
For there is something brave here. You see it

in the smoky red syrup that cools into shapes
of miniature soldiers, the backs that cannot bend.
With all the weather that scatters the words

of the broken vow, be the muscle, it says,
the sigh let go, the fisherman's sinker.
Be the blackened vault that survived the blaze,

the radiologist's apron across her heart.
Or the vat no flame of acid can corrode.
Be the man who returns to his bed at dawn,

the long deep breath that settles through the branches,
the ocean silt that forgives all things.
Across the milkweed of the battlefield,

beneath the sweep of the metal sensor,
be the sleepy gravity of all
the distant years of loss. Be here. At last.

Even as you walk. Beneath the hover
of the history seeker: the solder's grip,
the fallen thunder, the exhausted bullet.

The Invention of Fire

I cannot count the years it lay buried
in veins of flint beneath the Sangre de Christos,
safe from us, as we in turn were safe
from it, so that we might understand
so little about it, how lightning strikes
from both our skies, above us and below.
And beyond that, the hidden nature of things
bound us to them, to each other even,
like boys huddled about a fire, seeing
these bright gestures among the trees as one
more threshold that fluttered in the wind,
the air full of smoke, talk, stars to sleep by,
men with hooks who slashed the night down
the sternum to reveal and conceal
at once this gift, this heart we cannot touch.

II.

Ground Zero

My father slept through the great collapse,
through news that fired up a billion rooms,

a billion insomniac televisions compulsive
with disaster. He slept through prayers

morning would find him conscious, looking
down at the thin blue gown, like a man

from a steep cliff who sees his future there.
And through the hours that ground us into salt,

he slept inside our sleep, everywhere
the soot we breathed, slow to fall completely,

if it ever did, above the quiet embers.
He slept the way a coal sleeps, cloaked

in ash, our hands held out to feel the center,
drawn inward by the hospital chill.

And so, later, when he finally woke,
his language in pieces, we kept it all secret,

how the world had changed, as he too kept
his journey to himself. Or from himself.

Who were we to know, we who conceived
our history in terms of travel, in absence

of a traveler. Light, as we knew it, went
so far against the scorched earth, no farther.

No angel over the opening. Only smoke.
And inside that, the memory of smoke,

the great tide that made it hard to see,
to look back at our towers as we ran.

The News

Which is the greater mercy, she asks,
to know your husband has a month,
maybe two, or to go on gliding
over nightfall as a last bird,
a hope on a string, bobbing
in the wind that bears you up.
It's only now, a year gone,
she discovers what he held
back, what he trapped in his lung
where it darkened their lives,
as if to grant in good faith
a red star inside the blindness.
Which is the greater burden,
a sudden shock when it comes
or the cling of the living arm.
What is the blue light of day
by day compared to the bitter
bread they might have broken.
And now, this news, late, this gift
he never meant to be given.
It is another meal she shares
with no one, another anger
that turns toward death and back
over and over, until rage
exhausts itself in charity,
in sleep. That was his intent,
she imagines, the goodness of sleep
he saw beside him, seated, alone,
watching as her life rose
softly in her chest, breath by breath,
rose and settled, rose and settled.

Tinnitus

for John Tait

What is a past if not a body
that follows you from room to room,

the music of your childhood
spun at volumes so enflamed,

you cannot hear your neighbors
pounding back. To be blown

by winds that blur the eyes of woofers,
that strip you of your shirt, your name,

your hours of boredom, isn't this
what you wanted, to dissolve

the way a tab of x dissolves
into the sea of mind it opens.

All the nights you surfed the waters
of the mosh pit, grown older in it,

all those hands you trusted to hold
you up, afloat the anonymity

of touch. Noise is the other silence,
especially now, as the damage

in your head grows worse at night.
So little to mask the quiet siren

that is not there. Somewhere, it says,
there is a stranger who needs you

the way a past needs a future
to breathe, to bear it out of danger.

And so you turn on an old TV
with no one in it, just the soft

white hiss that is less than nothing,
more than anything, that becomes

your erasure, yours and everyone's.
Not the hoarse voice of thousands,

but the thousands at a distance,
out there where a boy might collapse

on the dance floor, in trauma, in joy,
or both at once, his heart seized

with the thrill of a hundred hammers,
and the crowd raves on, with eyes

of an emergency, and the bass drum
of the sky-wall shatters into stars.

Horn

My mother sits befuddled at her telephone,
uncertain who she means to call
or why, which pill was the one
she feared she took.
Her dial tone is a tiny car,
its driver asleep, leaning on the horn.

These broken nights, when rest comes
late or not at all, her voice
gets lower, rougher, her father's voice
emerging in her own.
One more day, she tells herself,
though what she is approaching she could not say.

And in time it comes, the mercy
of the empty places. In time
her mind gives out like headlights
over the darkened water. *Closer*,
I tell my mother, and she gazes up,
bemused, and down again;

hold the receiver closer, closer,
the phone's grid of little figures
looking back. So foreign to her now,
this belly full of numbers
sparked and glowing, this far alarm
pulsing in her hand.

Jahrzeit

Not that the dead care
what day we remember,

if we touch a silent match
to history and watch

it pull against the wick,
the flame a past that wakes

again and again, a man
who can't quite understand

where he is. Or who.
What we cannot know

we give a date, a place,
the missing part of us

we see now everywhere,
though who's to say it's there

until the candle makes
it so, until this smoke

signs the atmosphere.
Earth turns and so turns over

some dull and weary shovel
that cannot grieve them all.

Death too is growing old.
And strangely it's the child

who talks to things that burn,
waiting for an answer.

It's the trance of those
who sit motionless

in dying rooms and stare
into the candle's star,

thinking it's their story
now, their body's body,

their dim sight year by year
passing through the fire.

The Ghost of Weather

A man takes smaller steps
in his eighties, his body leaning
slightly forward as if against
a continuous wind. He turns
and the wind turns with him,
the impoverished rumor of it
always in his face, blearing
his eyes, bothering his ears.

There's no way around it,
this ghost of weather thrown
out of the world, rushing
through the gape of doors,
so much farther than they were,
over the still flowers of curtains
and chairs, through the window
sealed like an anxious letter,

so that floors expand, the way
years between the stars expand,
taking on the dimensions
he remembers as a child.
It's as if all things, retreating
from each other, return
to a nameless place, light
as paper boats, as prayers.

Words too have a way of scattering
in the mind, of coming loose,
burning in the night's great sea of ink.
Look, there, where the jaws

of the book open to yawn
or swallow, to take him in.
Look, as he dips his sleepy head
with only the wind to catch it.

Wind

Long ago, the names we gave it blew
over our tongues, over those who saw
not wind precisely but what it moved,

to flesh a thing that was not a thing,
more a blur, like us, and so beyond us.
And though in time the syllables changed,

the dead tongues were in there somewhere,
they still are, not to mention the mothers
who handed them down, a little rain

in their voices falling over the roof,
over children in their beds who heard
in them skies fall to put their fears to sleep.

Today my wife can barely talk. She looks
instead to the details of a mother's
memorial, to music, prayers, final debts.

All of us this day have our distractions.
With or without them, we look away.
The north blows against the temple bells.

Just where it starts is anyone's guess,
the current and the word that carries it.
No end to the words we bring to words

to open them, the words we bring to silence.
And yet we get just so many before
the day that gives them a number. Hard,

tangible, this number, and clear as wind.
So difficult to break a mother's code
as it in turn breaks down. A last wish

perhaps, a private word, as if language
could still be language and hers alone.
The dead tongues are in there somewhere,

the words a child hears before words.
Long ago the sound of my wife's name
rose and fell into the dark cradle.

Good night, said the world crackling with wind.
Good night, said the word for wind, and breath,
cascading inward, deepened to a roar.

The Lost Year

After the storm, when the wind pulled down
all that was high and dying from the trees,
when the north blew out the candle of our home,
our roof chipped, gutters flooded, it seemed
so unlikely, the calm that followed, the strength
of blue, the kind of quiet a room possesses
after a banquet. Clouds passed like ships on fire.

And I thought of the lost year, the one
of the gaping summer, the tentative one
that opened up your body like a question.
Tell me if you can. What has the flesh taught you
in its difficult season. There are days,
no doubt, that turn away the gift of knowledge
like a parcel with a clock inside.

Still you must admit. The road feels more
spacious now, though more solitary,
more uncertain. Stars gem the damaged branches.
They clarify the gaps between. These nights
you tug a little darkness to your chin.
But then, what do I know. Only the space
of not knowing, how near it is and always.

You dip your spoon into a bowl of milk
to row across the white pool.
You of all people understand
the blessings of appetite. You gape, you swallow,
and the world keeps moving through you.
It is the wind in the torch, the blood in the muscle.
Go on, it says. Even without knowing
now, you die a little into joy.

III.

Once

All stories begin in the middle
and likewise end there, pressed
for time, again, as we all are.
Once I knew a woman who woke
from surgery to her son's
gaze, her face full of questions
for the husband who, years before
while he was sleeping, died.

A larger story lived inside
the one she was in. It always
does. Imagine the confusion
when the son gently broke
the news and the husband died
again. If a self is made
of stories, who is telling them.
I ask myself sometimes.

Who is the one that suffers another
closure, as if dying were less
singular now. This morning
I opened the door of my eye
to search the clock for the hours
behind me. For a moment my house
was not my house. What luck,
to return, a changed man, to you,
my stranger. And then, and then.

Chimera

The better the book, the more of us it reads.
Even as I look away, words float
across a world I never knew was there.

Page after page, I feel the light wind
breathe a little sense into things.
Why would it be any different with you.

I knew a man once who had one blue iris,
another green. Sisters, he called them,
born into the womb through separate lives,

each a sacrament eaten by the other.
When he talked, I wondered which of his
to answer, though that was my own eye talking.

There are those who believe we learn nothing
outside of what we know, as if wisdom
were a shovel, a hole. I have buried too much

to go there, to see time as motionless
as numbers, or claim, as numbers do, all things
die into memory where they await us.

Was it the me or I who led to this.
I want to say neither. My father taught me
to behave, and I loved that about him.

Sometimes he was cross at the table,
and we crumpled into tears. If he talked
when we were talking, our voices vanished.

A lot of books feel that way, I know.
The day he died, it set certain limits
the way a father does. If I say I visit

his body still, blame it on the twin stars.
Disbelief has eyes of different colors.
So dark, this ink, this emptiness between.

Memento

Beneath your eyelid trembling with sleep,
below the fire there, the burning leaves
where they blindly gesture, move your lip,

flare up beside the father, say, alive
now in the oak grove of your childhood,
what you don't see is everything a life

of exhaustion drains away like old blood,
how dreaming is the color that takes out
the memory you cannot use, the burden

of hours unredeemed by dread or want.
Who wouldn't stare at the brighter phase,
hardly breathing, gilded by the cold light.

Not just the force of what these branches raise.
Not the mere shine of leaves you see inside
the blighted clearing of a father's face.

It's the appetite of flames you need,
how it simplifies the kindling as it breaks,
as it crackles like the nearing feet

of an animal drawn out of the dark.
To see your father now, you must give away
a piece of something, of you, of him, these oaks

perhaps, the dying embers of the day.
It could be grief, this thing that brings you closer
to your beginnings. Even as you wake,

it sheds something of its blaze, its power,
something of the man who once stirred the grave
of light with a stick. 'Til it too caught fire.

Convalescence

*There's 29,000 people in the ballpark
and a million butterflies.*

— VIN SCULLY

As a boy, I drowned in my infections
and lay beside my bedroom window, as Kio,
our gardener, my friend, took his shears

to our view of heaven, in his mouth
a Camel, in his pocket a Dodger game,
a 3-2 pitch, Vin Scully at the mike.

Even those at the game brought radios
to hear buried in the action a cadence
of highs and lows, the tug of the cap,

the shrug, the kid who eyed the bag at first,
each present tense so sharply rendered
it felt, strangely, chiseled, crisp, the stuff

of a future past. How reassuring,
to gaze into the leaves of our avocado
and spy there some opening between

the fielders where a triple might drop
its news to send us into extra innings.
The voice we heard was a pair of eyes,

the kind that sees what is and is not quite there,
not yet, just enough of the possible
to sweat it out, to be the child again,

knowing a game is just that, and so
a thing that tests our faith, good and bad,
where a legend taps the plate in prayer.

For that moment we did the same, given
how Kio muttered his encouragement
through his cigarette, coughing a bit,

looking the future dead in the eye to make
light whatever it was: the work, the worry,
the wait. All of us were butterflies,

or lost among them, thanks to the inflection
broadcast live, where our heroes fell
in time like branches. A swing and a miss.

Each out cleared space for the next at bat,
behind in the count, where a man becomes
what he is to a boy: a boast, a coward,

a master of flying objects, possessed
by fate and heart to crack the sweet spot
of the sky, and hit it out of the park.

Cyclops

My first memory is a hero's journey.
I am watching a movie of ancient Greeks
at the mercy of their script, my father

beside me in the dark, in the Crown
Theater warm with bodies, as somewhere
above us the one-eye of the projector

flutters and hums, the father of us all.
Too small to disbelieve the extremes
of what I do and do not trust, I am

sailing through the surface of the screen,
until it is my body, my suit of armor,
my head in the mouth of the monster

as he wipes his lip. I have a skin
too delicate to hold me, to shield me
from the great pupil, the cry, the thread

of drool as the camera looks away.
For all I know, this is my necessary
nightmare, the dread that spears the eye

it opens. A birth, although I see it still,
the way I whimper like an animal,
how my father leads me to the sunlight

of the lobby, the broad day as it burns
down the trance and everyone inside it.
What my dad says there, I don't recall,

though I picture somewhere in the glass
door the Crown Theater of a world
outside, as if it were a second father.

A monster knows no father but himself.
I see that now. I imagine his eye
as a kind of island in a movie

that no one sees. Only the mantra
of the waves that eat into the known shore.
I take that mantra with me when I go

places my body will not go. Some nights
I repeat the number one in silence
to fall asleep. Slowly the rock crumbles.

The sail rustles into bloom. Some nights
I am a child in my own arms.
There is a larger world. And it is this one.

Boo

Or so says the mother who gives her child
a scare, or rather a tiny theater
of scares, an unexpected laugh to scatter
the mask of her fingers, to make the world
the mended mirror of her face, the first,
as the years will tell him, he learns to miss,
to mystify with a prospect of loss,
a silent promise that never goes missing.
It survives. And what could be better
than the little thrills they give each other.
For without the seeing that believes,
our sun lost behind the curtain, the day
goes headless, when out of nothing it arrives,
ablaze, to break the windows of our eyes.

The Collector

Blame the past, if you must, the child
inside the man. Blame his hungry eye
for things, his pupil like a small black coin.
And while we are at it, blame the coin,
the one that feeds his appetite, that turns

the pages in a chronicle of coins,
their rows laid out like plates before a banquet.
It reminds me of the face that calms
the child, pressing there a symmetry
of eyes he will carry in his own.

There's milk in that gaze, thinks the child.
There's a mirror driven through the flesh,
to each the silent echo of the other.
And soon a courtship, a peek-a-boo that flirts
with the fear of echoes disappearing.

A courtship in the restoration of all
that matters, of matter, of mother, a courtship still
unsure of what it courts, of the want
that overflows the chamber of the eye.
Soon it's everywhere: *lust*, as in *luster.*

Not that the collector defies the end
of mothers, mirrors, eyes. Or that the mere
blaze of shiny objects might reify
the loss. But loss and wonder become sister
stars that pull each other into orbit.

So it is with nostalgia and greed.
How sweet the prize he slips into the green
felt of sleeves and boxes, their little holes.
It makes him feel less shameful, to sleep
on his stomach with his back to the world.

Pride, sure, but even more the fond illusion
of arrival, as if to open a book of coins,
a complete set, no less, was to close
a door, a wing, a musical phrase.
It begs him to open and shut again, again

until the book becomes a bird that knows
no rest, no land, no instinct but its own.
Do the faces of the gods find their beauty
unbearable at times. Does the metal
of them ache, here below the river of eyes

that washes over the collection, careful
not to rub the dates from the coins,
the boredom from the statesman, the fire
from the torch. Every token a wish
passed down to here, now, its final respite.

Perhaps we take away the awe of that.
Or see in each page the hopelessness
of hope suspended, unspent. Ever lifeless
and alive, the stuff of chance, isn't that
what coins are. It makes the greatest prize

the worthless, the priceless, the one you keep.
Somewhere in the miniature parade
of dimes, the heads of Mercury transfigure
into presidents, into the keys
of a piano built to raise the dead.

The good gods are back there somewhere.
And at the center of their great design,
a glorious nothing. Not mystery.
More like outer space, that weightlessness
that spins the heavy matter of our things.

If this makes the collector an idealist,
then he is an angel among angels.
A glorious nothing. Like the tear-drop shot
that wins the game. Sweet whisper of the zero
inside the net. *I am,* it says, repeating.

I will be, and one by one the hearts fall
out of the sky like birds, slow to return
to the bones of the nest. We shuffle home.
A cup scuttles the abandoned aisle.
And it is quiet there. Still there is something

miraculous in the hush that slides
its window over things, in the seascape
that casts a silence over what it sees,
what it loves, over the collector even.
There are motives so soft he may not hear them.

I don't know. For while the children walk
ruffled there against the shoreline breezes,
while the wind we see never blows
and never blows away; beneath the lather
of the tide and its constant reaching,

he feels a strange release. Not merely
from the ache of blue or what the lip
of water says. But from meaning itself.
As if to own were to disown. To disavow.
To let the wings inside the gilded frame

sweep the exaltation of the surf
that is wild, anxious, dispossessed.
The wheat, the god, the buffalo, the shine—
all dream of us. With his magnifying
lens in hand, the collector bows his head.

It's how he imagines the dead look,
drifting over us in their glass boats.
What we see at stake, it is the smoke
and polish of eyes as they pass, the surge
of matter as it wanders to the ocean.

The books close again, again at our feet,
at this place where it all began, they say,
the life we know so little about, the heart
that beats against the shore. I love the sea
with its power both to trouble and soothe,

to open the gate of sleep. Magnanimous
collector of the world, its skulls, its pearls,
its enameled spirals, the luminous fish.
Not to mention the black rake of the wave
drawing back, the moon-pull, the hunt,

the release, the grind and refinement
of all that lies below, older than the gods,
their torch, their banner, old as earth itself,
as the rain that breaks across the mirror,
the clouds that tumble as the waters rise.

About Bruce Bond

After receiving degrees in English from Pomona College and Claremont Graduate School, Bruce Bond earned his MA in Music Performance from Lamont School of Music. For several years then he worked as a classical and jazz musician in Colorado, after which he went on to receive his PhD in English from the University of Denver. His previous collections of poetry include *The Visible* (LSU, 2012), *Peal* (Etruscan, 2009), *Blind Rain* (Finalist, The Poets' Prize; LSU, 2008), *Cinder* (Etruscan Press, 2003), *The Throats of Narcissus* (University of Arkansas, 2001), *Radiography* (TIL Best Book of Poetry Award, BOA Editions, 1997), *The Anteroom of Paradise* (Colladay Award; QRL, 1991), and *Independence Days* (R. Gross A ward; Woodley Press, 1990). His poetry has appeared in *Best American Poetry*, *The Yale Review*, *The Georgia Review*, *Raritan*, *The New Republic*, *The Virginia Quarterly*, *Poetry*, and many other journals, and he has received numerous honors including fellowships from the NEA, Texas Commission on the Arts, The Institute for the Advancement of the Arts, and other organizations. Presently he is Regents Professor of English at the University of North Texas and Poetry Editor for American *Literary Review*.

Books from Etruscan Press

The Shyster's Daughter | Paula Priamos
Saint Joe's Passion | JD Schraffenberger
Lies Will Take You Somewhere | Sheila Schwartz
Fast Animal | Tim Seibles
American Fugue | Alexis Stamatis
The Casanova Chronicles | Myrna Stone
The White Horse: A Colombian Journey | Diane Thiel
The Fugitive Self | John Wheatcroft

Etruscan Press Is Proud of Support Received From

Wilkes University

Youngstown State University

The Raymond John Wean Foundation

The Ohio Arts Council

The Stephen & Jeryl Oristaglio Foundation

The Nathalie & James Andrews Foundation

The National Endowment for the Arts

The Ruth H. Beecher Foundation

The Bates-Manzano Fund

The New Mexico Community Foundation

The Gratia Murphy Endowment

Founded in 2001 with a generous grant from the Oristaglio Foundation, Etruscan Press is a nonprofit cooperative of poets and writers working to produce and promote books that nurture the dialogue among genres, achieve a distinctive voice, and reshape the literary and cultural histories of which we are a part.

etruscan press
www.etruscanpress.org

Etruscan Press books may be ordered from

Consortium Book Sales and Distribution
800.283.3572
www.cbsd.com

Small Press Distribution
800.869.7553
www.spdbooks.org

Etruscan Press is a 501(c)(3) nonprofit organization.
Contributions to Etruscan Press are tax deductible
as allowed under applicable law.
For more information, a prospectus,
or to order one of our titles,
contact us at books@etruscanpress.org.